# The Travels of Media and Cultural Products

This book presents the Cultural Transduction framework as a conceptual tool to understand the processes that media and cultural products undergo when they cross cultural and national borders.

Using a series of examples from pop culture, including films, television series, video games, memes and other digital products, this book provides the reader with a wider understanding of the procedures, interests, roles, assumptions and challenges, which foster or hinder the travels of media and cultural products. Compiling in one single narrative a series of case studies, theoretical debates and international examples, the book looks at a number of exchanges and transformations enabled by both traditional media trade and the internet. It reflects on the increase of cultural products crossing over regional, national and international borders in the form of video games and TV formats, through music and video distribution platforms or via digital social media networks, to highlight discussions about the characteristics of border-crossing digital production.

The cultural transduction framework is developed from discussions in communication and media studies, as well as from debates in adaptation and translation studies, to map out the travels of media and cultural products from an interdisciplinary perspective. It provides a tool to analyse the markets, products, people and processes that enable or constrain the movement of products across borders, for those interested in the practical aspects that underlie the negotiation and transformation of products inserted into different cultural market settings. This volume provides a new framework for understanding the travels of cultural products, which will be of use to students and scholars in the area of media industry studies, business studies, digital media studies, international media law and economics.

**Enrique Uribe-Jongbloed** (PhD Aberystwyth University) is research associate for Media Cymru, a UKRI Strength in Places Fund programme-funded project, at Cardiff University and professor researcher at the School of Social Communication and Journalism, Universidad Externado de Colombia. He has always worked at the crossroads of culture, language, identity and media production. He is a founding member of the International Association for Minority Language Media Research and member of the editorial board of the journals *Palabra Clave* and *Journal of Digital Media and Policy*. His most recent publications include co-editing the collections *Indigenous Language for Development Communication in the Global South* (2022) and *Indigenous Language for Social Change Communication in the Global South* (2023), and co-authoring the book *Los Trabajadores Colombianos del Cine Internacional* (2021).

# Routledge Studies in Media and Cultural Industries

For more information about this series,please visit: https://www.routledge.com/
Routledge-Studies-in-Media-and-Cultural-Industries/book-series/RSMCI

# The Travels of Media and Cultural Products

## Cultural Transduction

**Enrique Uribe-Jongbloed**

Routledge
Taylor & Francis Group

LONDON AND NEW YORK

First published 2024
by Routledge
4 Park Square, Milton Park, Abingdon, Oxon OX14 4RN

and by Routledge
605 Third Avenue, New York, NY 10158

*Routledge is an imprint of the Taylor & Francis Group, an informa business*

© 2024 Enrique Uribe-Jongbloed

The right of Enrique Uribe-Jongbloed to be identified as author of this work
has been asserted in accordance with sections 77 and 78 of the Copyright,
Designs and Patents Act 1988.

*British Library Cataloguing-in-Publication Data*
A catalogue record for this book is available from the British Library

*Library of Congress Cataloging-in-Publication Data*
Names: Uribe-Jongbloed, Enrique, author.
Title: The travels of media and cultural products : cultural transduction /
by Enrique Uribe-Jongbloed.
Description: New York : Routledge, 2024. | Series: Routledge studies in
media and cultural industries | Includes bibliographical references and index. |
Identifiers: LCCN 2023027537 (print) | LCCN 2023027538 (ebook) |
ISBN 9781032460345 (hardback) | ISBN 9781032461427 (paperback) |
ISBN 9781003380221 (ebook)
Subjects: LCSH: Mass media and culture. | Cultural industries . | Mass
media—Marketing.
Classification: LCC P94.6 U75 2024 (print) | LCC P94.6 (ebook) |
DDC 302.23—dcundefined
LC record available at https://lccn.loc.gov/2023027537
LC ebook record available at https://lccn.loc.gov/2023027538

ISBN: 978-1-032-46034-5 (hbk)
ISBN: 978-1-032-46142-7 (pbk)
ISBN: 978-1-003-38022-1 (ebk)

DOI: 10.4324/9781003380221

Typeset in Times New Roman
by codeMantra

To the memory of the academic rockstar that left us way too soon, my friend, co-author, and intellectual sparring partner, Sergio Roncallo-Dow.

Wherever you may be, it is always *Miércoles de Rock!*

# Contents

# Figures

# Tables

# Boxes

# Foreword

## Ten years building a clearer picture

Dr. Hernan David Espinosa-Medina
Digital Project Manager and Designer
Atmo Biosciences
ORCID 0000–0002–3561–4016

TV came to Colombia in 1953, and Colombian creators immediately began producing and developing content with a personal and unique style. Very quickly, these creators started exploring and generating a language with which they could imprint the particularities of their context, connecting audiences to content uniquely and almost personally. An example of this exploration could be the adaptation of regional literature and stories and the portrayal of characters and scenes by creators like Martha Bossio. However, from the beginning, TV was also a place to bring stories from other times and places to Colombian viewers. For instance, Bernardo Romero Lozano developed Tele-Teatro ("Tele-theatre"). In this show, Romero and his company adapted for the screen works of international writers like Kafka, Arthur Miller, and various Greek tragedies.

As time went by, this exploration took other shapes and forms. Telenovelas, a specific daily dramatic format that narrated long plots throughout 200–300 episodes, became a staple of Latin American TV, and Colombia became a production powerhouse of the genre. By the 1980s and 1990s, Mexico, Venezuela, Argentina, and others commonly imported and exported telenovelas among themselves and abroad. In that environment, Colombian creators learnt to compete with their foreign counterparts to reach audiences that, though similar to Colombians, remained different and distinctive.

Similarly, other countries started finding ways to bring their productions inside Colombian borders. For example, Japan exported multiple children's shows translated into Spanish. Furthermore, by the late 1990s, cable and satellite TV massively brought shows from the US to an audience that, up until then, had only limited access to that content. At this time, the Simpsons suddenly spoke Spanish through dubbing magic. Similarly, creators were called upon to close caption the humour of Seinfeld and Friends so that Jerry and Chandler could reach people that had only seen the big apple on a screen and in photographs.

Meanwhile, films took months or even years to reach the theatres of Bogota, Santiago, Lima, and the rest of the continent. This delay resulted from the arduous work of translation and how distributors had to negotiate exhibition rights that matched their expectations for international revenue. Even back then, international distribution represented an enormous opportunity to expand the revenue of their box office. Finding the right timing and strategy for reaching each market was crucial for these distributors, and it took cunning and finesse to find out the best way to reach and exploit each market. The politics and business of film distribution were a ruthless game that opened as many doors as it closed. Exclusivity and package deals meant that some films would reach the audience while others would have to wait decades to reach them by cable or streaming, if they ever did at all. Even the distribution of European or Latin American films was submitted to the might of the US distributors, and many voices seemed destined to never reach audiences beyond the esoteric showings of some film school classrooms.

Similar music, comic books, and other recorded media stories could be told. Stories where politics and censorship played a role, for example. For instance, we could tell the story of a law that taxed the importation of periodic publications to Colombia to curb the sale of pornography which defined periodical publications so broadly that it ended up completely restricting access to comic books within the country's borders. Alternatively, we could tell the stories of how fans of Japanese *anime* had to go to great ordeals to create VHS copies of their films with homemade subtitles, building an underground market of films that more than distributed where almost passed as a secret hand by hand from their origin in the far east to many living rooms in the tropic. These underground markets meant that many Colombian children of the 1990s played games on the Nintendo Famicom system instead of the Nintendo Entertainment System (NES) distributed in the US. Because of this apparently small difference in access, these children played games that displayed entire dialogues in Kanji, Hiragana, and Katakana characters instead of Spanish or even English. Translation and meaning were then left to the kids' imagination and how they interpreted gameplay.

I mention these stories because they lay at the heart of the research that originated many of the ideas that Enrique renders in this book. In 2013 Enrique came to me with an apparently simple question, "How do audiovisual products travel between cultural markets?" As a Colombian who had grown up in the world described above, he felt it was essential to understand this question so that content producers could appreciate how to reach faraway places to share their voices with the world and expand their chances of making a living out of their labour. The question was enthralling, and in the years since, it has opened a million avenues of exploration that have slowly started to form a clear picture.

Was the movement of products a question of translation? Was it a matter of geopolitics or business? What role did interpretation and adaptation play in the movement of products? Who were the critical gatekeepers and decision-makers that decided what products would reach different markets? What were their methods for reaching peoples all over the world?

Of course, we were not the first to ask such questions. In our first effort to understand this matter, we found great reflections on the role of power in the negotiations that underlay the movement of cultural products (Appadurai, 1990; Straubhaar, 1991, 2010). We discovered how others tried to describe product flows within markets (Moran, 2009a, 2009b, 2009c). Some researchers described the creative strategies creators used to reach foreign viewers. Some tried to understand if there was a way to reach a global audience with culturally odourless narratives (Olson, 1999). Others investigated how products were localised (Moran, 2009b; Pym, 2004) to help audiences grasp the content more easily. Yet others looked at a combination of both (Wang & Yeh, 2005). In these explorations, some researchers tried to understand how producers and creators could exploit cultural similarities and proximities to reach audiences. Alternatively, how they could understand distance and differences to avoid alienating the people, they expected to reach (La Pastina & Straubhaar, 2005; Rohn, 2011).

Moreover, other areas seemed filled with insights that spoke to these questions, even though they were not necessarily speaking about products reaching beyond national and regional borders. Translation studies highlighted essential considerations on preserving meaning even when languages sometimes radically differ. Adaptation studies explored many subjects regarding the importance of context and the particularities of different media and environments.

All these works and areas, and more, seemed to each contribute a vital piece of the puzzle. However, they did not seem to fit together. Theories and works were sometimes built on common grounds or entered into dialogue with others. However, many of these areas were more often separated and appeared to ignore each other. Moreover, their terms and vocabularies collided and were not always compatible, making constructing connections between them challenging.

Hence the task was straightforward, we needed to build a framework that helped bridge the concepts and ideas into a coherent description and then explore the pertinence of this model as a descriptor of real life to refine it based on as much evidence as we could collect. That was the start of the journey in 2013, and in 2014 we produced our first attempt at such a framework; cultural transduction (Uribe-Jongbloed & Espinosa-Medina, 2014).

Since then, many have contributed, criticised, reframed, examined, refined, and expanded the ideas we first attempted to bring together. More impressively,

Enrique has remained steadfast in absorbing ideas, participating in the debate, articulating new concepts and encouraging new voices to continue the exploration. Not only that, but the picture has continued to evolve and mutate beyond anything we could have expected: Streaming, international treaties and incentives, the movement of geopolitics and interests. Through all of these, Enrique has made his best effort to keep the work on cultural transduction updated and relevant.

This book is not just a consolidation of all the lessons learnt but a monumental effort to synthesise the hallmarks of their evolution, so that the exploration can keep building forward. The task will never be complete, and as long as creators keep creating, new horizons will be open for investigation. I hope that the work you have in your hands will spark curiosity and excitement and give you tools not just to understand better some of the nuances of how audiovisual products travel between cultural markets but that it inspires you to keep digging, taking these ideas where they have never gone before.

Beyond that, I bid you well in the land of cultural transduction you are about to enter. I know a small portion of the road you are about to travel, and I can tell you are in for a ride. Enjoy this excellent work.

## References

Appadurai, A. (1990). Disjuncture and difference in the global cultural economy. *Theory, Culture and Society*, 7(2), 295–310. https://doi.org/10.1177/026327690007002017

La Pastina, A. C., & Straubhaar, J. D. (2005). Multiple proximities between television genres and audiences: The schism between telenovelas' global distribution and local consumption. *International Communication Gazette*, 67(3), 271–288. https://doi.org/10.1177/0016549205052231

Moran, A. (2009a). *New flows in global TV*. Intellect.

Moran, A. (2009b). *TV formats worldwide: Localizing global programs*. Intellect.

Moran, A. (2009c). When TV formats migrate: The languages of business and culture. *Media International Australia*, 131, 16–29.

Olson, S. R. (1999). *Hollywood planet: Global media and the competitive advantage of narrative transparency*. Lawrence Erlbaum Associates, Inc.

Pym, A. (2004). The moving text. Localization, translation, and distribution. *America*, 12, 245.

Rohn, U. (2011). Lacuna or universal? Introducing a new model for understanding crosscultural audience demand. *Media Culture Society*, 33(4), 631–641. https://doi.org/10.1177/0163443711399223

Straubhaar, J. D. (1991). Beyond media imperialism: Asymmetrical interdependence and cultural proximity. *Critical Studies in Mass Comunication*, 8(1), 39–59.

Straubhaar, J. D. (2010). Chindia in the context of emerging cultural and media powers. *Global Media and Communication*, 6(3), 253–262. https://doi.org/10.1177/1742766510384962

Uribe-Jongbloed, E., & Espinosa-Medina, H. D. (2014). A clearer picture: Towards a new framework for the study of cultural transduction in audiovisual market trades. *Observatorio, 8*(1), 23–48. http://obs.obercom.pt/index.php/obs/article/view/707/642

Wang, G., & Yeh, E. Y. (2005). Globalization and hybridization in cultural products: The cases of Mulan and Crouching Tiger, Hidden Dragon. *International Journal of Cultural Studies, 8*(2), 175–193. https://doi.org/10.1177/1367877905052416

# Preface

This book is aimed at all levels of academics and practitioners interested in understanding how media and cultural products travel between locales. It strives to be easy to read even for those who are not used to academic writing. It is presented in short chapters that include box texts with detailed examples of each of the aspects mentioned. The evidence selected in the chapters is drawn from academic publications from all regions of the world. However, there are more examples stemming from Latin America than elsewhere. The reason for this is twofold. On the one hand, it is where I have developed most of my expertise. On the other, it seeks to provide examples beyond the Euro-American axis that are more prominent in the literature. Similarly, some of the texts included in the references are in languages other than English, hoping to bring attention to other academic approaches as part of the international focus of the book.

There is also a conscious effort to include different types of media products in the examples, ranging from TV shows to video games and memes. The idea was to expand the framework beyond the original focus on television formats, which is still the central structure of the concept and the book. It is not easy to find appropriate examples from all forms of media products, but hopefully there is sufficient breadth in the ones selected to provide an overview of how this framework seeks to cover them.

Cultural transduction has been a topic I have been keen to develop in the last ten years and I considered it is time to make it into a concise volume, rather than a collection of published articles scattered in journals. The main interest was to provide a single narrative that would include sufficient examples, ample references, and enough material to invite other academics to engage with the concept.

The way the book is organised begins with a chapter describing how the concept of cultural transduction came to be and how the framework was developed. Each of the four following chapters describes in detail the tenets of the framework, providing examples and definitions of related concepts that have been incorporated. Finally, the last chapter offers guidelines on how to use the framework as an analytic tool or as a step-by-step process to assess the values and requirements for successful transduction.

The main goal of this shortform book is to bring the attention to the concept, promote its application, critique, and development, improve its structure and usability for future endeavours to comprehend, and promote the travels of cultural and media products beyond cultural borders. I am sure there is much to improve. I acknowledge my limitations and admit responsibility for all the shortcomings, mistakes, and inaccuracies of this book. Yet I rest satisfied knowing that future scholarly developments on this field will build upon the merits found within these pages.

# Acknowledgements

There are many people who have contributed profoundly to the development of this book.

First and foremost, my friend and colleague, Dr. Hernán Espinosa-Medina, with whom the concept of Cultural Transduction was originally developed and researched. Without all the work, discussions, debates, and research we engaged with together, it would have never been possible to come to the point of publishing this book, almost ten years after our original article on the subject. Although it still saddens me that he was not able to join me in the preparation and development of the book, his contribution to the concept in our previous works has been central to the arguments that are presented here.

My colleagues, co-authors, and friends, Prof. Toby Miller, Dr. Daniel Aguilar-Rodriguez, Manuel A. Corredor-Aristizábal, César Mora Moreo, Dr. Carlos Gutiérrez González, Dr. Edward Goyeneche-Gómez, Alessandra Puccini Montoya, Dr. Manuel González-Bernal, Dr. Germán Arango-Forero, Dr. Ethel Pis Diez, and, obviously, Dr. Sergio Roncallo-Dow, all discussed with me, heard me babble about, or embraced the concept of cultural transduction, and each of them has added something to this development. I would also like to thank lecturers and friends at Universidad Externado de Colombia, Universidad de La Sabana, and Universidad del Norte, for their continuous support in the development of the basis for this book.

Dr. Kyle Conway and Dr. Sarah Maitland have also been fundamental in providing dialogue and discussion that has permeated many aspects of this book. Since our first chats over a video call, and later through his participation in the Cultural Transduction conference, Kyle has always been supportive of the central argument for Cultural Transduction as a framework, even if he defines it as part of, or almost identical to, cultural translation. We will see if this work finally convinces him of the differences or, if not, prompts him to publish further discussions into why we should stick to cultural translation. Since Sarah also advocates for cultural translation, I am currently outnumbered. I hope that soon the three of us will be able to produce a book on this debate, as we have planned for quite a while.

xxvi  *Acknowledgements*

I also would like to acknowledge those who have provided their wisdom and insights through interviews, such as Gerson da Silva and his co-workers at *Ironhide Game Studio*, who gently provided three of the figures included; Daniel Samper Pizano, who is a living legend and a wealth of knowledge; Richard Pring, Sam Leigh and the team at *Wales Interactive* who, after a conversation at a pub, also provided valuable information and two of the figures for this book. I want to thank all the members of the team at *Media Cymru* and *Cardiff University*, as the more recent group of people that has continued to allow me to expand on this idea through fruitful conversations.

Finally, there are many others who have helped me, heard me, debated with me or, sometimes, proved me wrong, and whose encouragement has been fundamental for the development of the concepts and applications presented in these. I would like to thank Maria Angel Orjuela Morales, Dr. Santiago Marino, Dr. Ana Bizberge, Dr. Manuel Salge Ferro, Harvey Murcia Quintero, Omar Oróstegui Restrepo and Prof. Elin Haf Gruffydd Jones. I hope each of you sees how your support helped in the development of this book.

This work was supported by the UK Research and Innovation Strength in Places Fund project Media Cymru [grant reference SIPF99911].

# 1 What is cultural transduction?

It all started when I was watching television in Germany in 2005. I had tuned to Sat.1 at around 4pm and they were showing a contemporary drama about a young woman beginning employment in a fashion company. Quickly I realised I had seen that story before. The show was called *Verliebt in Berlin* (Sat.1, 2005–2006) and was eerily similar to *Yo soy Betty, la fea* (RCN, 1999–2001), a show I had watched occasionally when it was on RCN, one of the Colombian private free-to-air television channels, at the turn of the century. I knew that it had been broadcast elsewhere in the world, with subtitles or dubbed, but I had never imagined an adaptation of a Colombian telenovela in Germany.

A few years after that, while working with Jeronimo Rivera-Betancur at Universidad de La Sabana in Colombia, we decided to work on a book chapter on *Yo soy Betty, la fea* for a collection by colleagues from Universidad de Sevilla. The ensuing book chapter (Rivera-Betancur & Uribe-Jongbloed, 2012) tried to present a first comparison between the Colombian and the American version, *Ugly Betty* (ABC, 2006), the latter of which we had been able to acquire as DVDs. The fact that the adaptation and format trade of *Yo soy Betty, la fea* became such an academic interest (see Box 1.1.) following the international success of the show (see Miller, 2010), became a motor to better understand how a Colombian television show had made it to become a global hit.

I began looking for all the information I could gather on the success of Colombian telenovelas abroad and managed to convince a colleague, Hernán Espinosa-Medina, to join me on this research adventure. Pretty soon we discovered there had been many interesting advances made in media studies regarding the phenomenon, but they were all stemming from a variety of disciplines or academic perspectives that talked about the same things but used a different set of concepts to describe their studies. By developing the literature review on the matter, which eventually became an academic article (see Uribe-Jongbloed & Espinosa-Medina, 2014), we realised we had to come up with our own definitions or, better yet, we had refined the existing ones, to be able to study similar phenomena to that of *Yo soy Betty, la fea*.

Since we began our studies looking at *Yo soy Betty, la fea* in the terms of it being a telenovela and a TV format, these were the main avenues we explored.

DOI: 10.4324/9781003380221-1

---

**Box 1.1** *Yo soy Betty, la fea* **as a global phenomenon**

*Yo soy Betty, la fea* (RCN, 1999–2001) has commanded international attention since its debut in Colombia in 1999, through the trade of the finished product, whether in its original Spanish, with subtitles or dubbed into various languages, having been sold as a format for different versions all over the world, and finally becoming a success again in Colombia and the rest of Latin America when it was shown through Netflix between 2020 and 2022. Numerous academic papers and books have been devoted entirely to this case to show evidence of a quality product that has managed to overcome international barriers to position itself as a point of reference for Colombian television production and format trade. It would be impossible to mention all the documents that have discussed the show or any of its versions, but it is a main case study that has addressed all the tenets of Cultural Transduction. This selection is by no means exhaustive, and it only hopes to serve as a guide for those interested in one of the most successful cases of international audiovisual trade arising from outside the major international markets.

Adriaens, F., & Biltereyst, D. (2011). Glocalized telenovelas and national identities: A "textual cum production" analysis of the "Telenovelle" Sara, the flemish adaptation of Yo soy Betty, la fea. *Television & New Media, 13*(6), 551–567. https://doi.org/10.1177/1527476411427926

Conway, K. (2012). Cultural translation, global television studies, and the circulation of telenovelas in the United States. *International Journal of Cultural Studies, 15*(6), 583–598. https://doi.org/10.1177/1367877911422291

Fung, A., & Zhang, X. (2011). The Chinese ugly betty: TV cloning and local modernity. *International Journal of Cultural Studies, 14*(3), 265–276. https://doi.org/10.1177/1367877910391866

McCabe, J. & Akass, K. (Eds.) (2013). TV's betty goes global: from telenovela to international brand. I.B. Tauris.

Mikos, L., & Perrotta, M. (2012). Traveling style: Aesthetic differences and similarities in national adaptations of Yo soy Betty, la fea. *International Journal of Cultural Studies, 15*(1), 81–97. https://doi.org/10.1177/1367877911428116

Miller, J. L. (2010). Ugly betty goes global: Global networks of localized content in the telenovela industry. *Global Media and Communication, 6*(2), 198–217. https://doi.org/10.1177/1742766510373717

Moran, A. (2009). When TV formats migrate: The languages of business and culture. *Media International Australia, 131*, 16–29.

Murillo, S. & Escala, L. (2013). De Betty, la fea a ugly betty. Circulación y adaptación de narrativas televisivas. *Cuadernos.info, 33*, 99–112. https://doi.org/10.7764/cdi.33.531

Rivera-Betancur, J. L., & Uribe-Jongbloed, E. (2012). La Suerte de la Fea, muchas la desean: de Yo soy Betty, la Fea a Ugly Betty. In M. Pérez (Ed.), *Previously on* (pp. 825–842). Universidad de Salamanca.

Rivero, Y. M. (2003) The performance and reception of televisual "ugliness" in Yo soy Betty la fea. *Feminist Media Studies*, *3*(1), 65–81, https://doi.org/10.1080/1468077032000080130

From the telenovela perspective we started from the scholarly contributions arising from Jesús Martín Barbero's (1987) seminal work *De los medios a las mediaciones* [From media to mediations], but they were mostly concerned with questions of representation within the national distribution of telenovelas, an area of work with considerable academic production in Latin America. They were often set under critical perspectives following Dorfman and Mattelart's (1998) classical re-reading of Donald Duck, and criticised the expansion of American media as an example of cultural imperialism. Telenovelas were presented as the way Latin America was responding to the cultural imposition of aesthetics and representations by providing our own national frames of reference (Martín Barbero, 2005; Mato, 2005). The premise was, as Tunstall (1977) had presented it, that *media are American*, and thus, television products were conveying an American way of life, that was disconnected to the experience in Latin America. This idea of a unidirectional flow of production and cultural values seemed somehow counterintuitive, since television channels in Colombia presented shows from other countries, including Mexico, Argentina, Venezuela, the UK, France, Germany, Japan, and even Australia. So, although it was clear that the US had a great presence in the Colombian small screen, it was by no means the only source of media production or the only form of representation people would have the opportunity to experience. There were a variety of locally produced shows including entertainment, drama, comedy, and current affairs widely throughout the 1970s and 1980s, and though some of them had been developed as copies of foreign productions, most were originals or adaptations of Latin American and universal literature – the latter mainly of works whose copyright restrictions had elapsed (Espinosa-Medina & Uribe-Jongbloed, 2016). The presence of other Latin American TV shows, including Mexican, Brazilian, and Venezuelan telenovelas, showed that there was another type of exchange that was not flowing through from the US.

## First conceptual tool: Cultural proximity

A similar observation regarding the flow of telenovelas had led Straubhaar (1991) to contest the supposed unilateral dependence on US media and talk about an asymmetrical interdependence, showing that in Latin America telenovela consumption and trade included regional exchanges. First, he noticed that countries preferred nationally produced shows over imports but that they were receptive of those imported from other Latin American countries. He mentioned that the reason for this trade was the similitude in cultural traits between the different Latin American countries, which enabled their media products to be understood and travel between them. He called this characteristic cultural proximity, a concept he would continue to develop further (see LaPastina & Straubhaar, 2005; Straubhaar, 2007) to include similarities in taste based on different collective traits, such as class, cultural, and linguistic capital. Straubhaar (2021) has since added nuance to his original proposal regarding cultural proximity, acknowledging that

> even a general favorable disposition toward national production will not necessarily save it from competition by attractive imported programs, channels, or streaming options, especially when these come in genres historically underrepresented in national production, such as dramatic or comedy series, action adventure series, police and detective series, or feature films.
>
> (p. 31)

Thus, with cultural proximity, we had come across the first exploration of what enabled audiovisual products to travel beyond a national context. This made perfect sense to comprehend the expansion, within Latin America, of Mexican and Venezuelan telenovelas, but it did not seem to clarify why shows from other countries also made it to Colombia, or why some telenovelas managed to reach European nations. There were certainly other reasons that promoted or hampered the export or import of television products from one market to the next.

## Formatology and cultural translation

Apart from this perspective on telenovelas, there was another aspect that seemed interesting to understand how media products travel. It was the development of the area that would later be called formatology (Moran & Aveyard, 2014, p. 24). In this area of studies, the concern was the development, trade, and modification of audiovisual products as formats. Moran (2004, 2009, 2013), Esser (2010, 2013a, 2013b), and Chalaby (2011, 2012a, 2012b, 2015, 2016) had written extensively about this aspect of audiovisual trade and represented something interesting for the case of *Yo soy Betty, la fea* (see Box 1.1). Format studies were particularly interesting by addressing some of the most evident cases of multinational adaptations of global game and reality shows. Although their origins could be traced to exchanges between the US and the UK as early as the 1920s in sound broadcasting, and to the 1940s for television shows (Chalaby, 2012a), it was in the 1990s that the unscripted format trade became a global industry (Chalaby, 2011), followed by scripted formats in the mid-2000s (Chalaby, 2015). It is then clear that

> TV formats testify both to the globalisation of television and to its nationalisation or even localisation. English may well be the language of the

TV format industry, but the TV format culture chooses to speak in other idioms and accents.

(Moran, 2009, p. 27)

Thus, keeping discussions about the format trade of *Yo soy Betty, la fea*, became central to understanding how products travelled between markets.

Another article which spoke specifically about the format negotiations behind the transformation of *Yo soy Betty, la fea* into *Ugly Betty* seemed to have pointed us in the specific direction we were aiming. Conway (2012b) had studied this process by performing an analysis of trade publications covering its negotiations and debates. His angle was not directly from formatology, as he was addressing it from translation studies, and used the concept of cultural translation to encapsulate this debate. It had been clear since the beginning that translation was a central part of the phenomenon, but since we were looking at audiovisual products, and translation is often associated exclusively with the transfer between two or more named languages[1], it had not occurred to us that it would be a perspective to look for to understand these processes.

## Coming up with cultural transduction

We did not stop there when analysing all the various factors that played a role in the development of a common lexicon, and eventually the framework, but it was around this point when Hernán Espinosa-Medina and I felt the need to provide a name to the phenomenon we were studying. We were concerned with the traits of a product that made it travel from one country to the next – including those that were altered in some form when that happened, and the market conditions or characteristics that enabled the transition, but also the negotiation processes and strategies that had allowed for this transformation to take place.

We knew that the main issue had to be that this whole process implied some form of change or modification of a product, be it in the characteristic of the product itself or in separating central elements of the product from the cultural characteristics that might prevent it from achieving cultural proximity. We spoke about the essence of the product in contrast to its other defining traits. Formats, as I had experienced with the case of *Verliebt in Berlin*, remove enough cultural aspects to render the product acceptable to a different audience, but keep enough of the original that I was able to make the connection. The essence is what seems to be transferred and, depending on the way it moves between settings, it forgoes the remaining traits. Cultural translation, the concept used by Conway (2012a, 2012b) seemed to describe this process, but from our perspective, the common use of the term translation to refer, mainly, to the change from one spoken, sign or written formal language to another, seemed to limit the scope of the changes. Clearly, cultural translation expands the understanding of translation to address the fact that translation is not just a change of one code for another in a direct transposition. Further explorations on the concept of cultural translation make this even clearer (see Maitland, 2017; Conway, 2020). Yet, when we were debating it, we felt we needed a different concept to define what this process entails.

Next in line we had the concept of adaptation that has created its own niche in film and literature studies as adaptation studies. The transformation of media products from one type of work to another has been studied for a long time under this concept, and it has encompassed other media and products including video games, thematic parks and comics (Hutcheon, 2013). However, the main perception remains that adaptation is predominantly concerned with the transformation of literature or theatre to film (Elleström, 2017, p. 517). Furthermore, if translation seems to concentrate on the used language as the central element to analyse based on a normative view of correct transposition of meaning between source and target named languages, in the case of adaptation the central aspect is the comparison between the products in regard to the fidelity of the target to the source material (Hermansson, 2015). It is true that cultural translation has moved away from only concerning itself with the formal or normative linguistic differences between texts and has become more concerned with the role and agency, creative input and authorship of the translator (Conway, 2012a), and adaptation studies has included many voices arguing for a more holistic approach that includes the materiality and industrial side of the process (see Elliot, 2013; Murray, 2008, 2012; Engelstad, 2018; Sherry, 2016) and the relation of multiple texts and historical versions which provide contextual interpretations (Szwydky, 2023). However, for both fields of studies, these perspectives remain outliers of their respective research disciplines, and they still bear the brunt of the associations we had with their loaded concepts of translation and adaptation.

Then, how else could we define the process of the transformation or transposition of a product from one place to another, in a way that would incorporate those ideas, while at the same time being considerably different from them. After many discussions, Hernán Espinosa-Medina's background in sound engineering provided us with an interesting metaphor. Transduction refers, in physics, to the change in type of energy between different vessels, or "the act of changing energy from one form to another" (Cambridge dictionary, 2023). If energy is the essence of the product, as we mentioned before, the traits of its vessel or form may change – basically its external cultural characteristics. Since we borrowed the term from physics, we thought that it was necessary to add that the transformation was cultural in nature, similar to what had been done with translation. Although culture is another loaded term, we considered that it was important to highlight that the type of transduction taking place referred to elements such as language, values, customs, and sensibilities, rather than limited to technical aspects of the media in question. That is how cultural transduction became our leading concept.

## Cultural transduction as framework

Cultural transduction was a concept better understood as a framework to analyse diverse cases. We could apply it beyond a comparison of two versions of a single product and consider the whole environment in which the process takes place. Of course, the product and its changes remain relevant, but so do the markets through which the product moves, the people who were responsible for the transduction to happen in the first place and the institutions or the mechanics of how it came to be. Obviously, this concept is profoundly indebted to cultural translation – to the point that Conway (2020, p. xviii) has described cultural transduction as my personal term for it – and adaptation studies (see Cattrysse, 2017), and this is evident in the following chapters.

Although the original idea of taking the metaphor from physics to the social sciences seemed to make sense, it was important to consider whether the concept had been used in other fields of inquiry, and recognise in how far transduction still served as a main conduit of our conceptual endeavour. Indeed, López Charles (2008) had already undertaken a similar path to address the meaning of transduction and included two more meanings to the one we had settled on, one from genetics and another from semiotics. In genetics, transduction is the transfer of genetic material from one cell to another via a viral agent (Cambridge dictionary, 2023), whereas

> in semiotics, the term refers to the transmission and transformation processes that literary works go through in activities such as the incorporation of a literary text (or some of its parts) into another one, changing from one genre to another one (novel to theater, cinema, etc.), translating a text to foreign languages, etc.
>
> (López Charles, 2008, p. 1)

The semiotic meaning seems to account for the elements that we wanted to address, although both the physics and genetics metaphor were also quite helpful to understand the importance, not only of *what* happens to the product, but *why* it happens, under which circumstances or environments and through which enabling agents.

In a nutshell, cultural transduction encompasses all the elements that take place when a given cultural product, as in our initial example, the Colombian telenovela *Yo soy Betty, la fea*, moves on to a different setting, becoming *Verliebt in Berlin* in Germany. Basically, it is easy to imagine a variety of debates dealing with the market where it was produced, Colombia, and its destination, Germany; characteristics of the product that may have remained, the essence, or removed and altered, the vessel; the people who selected, traded and modified one product into the other; and the setting through which the whole process took place, in this case referring to television format trades carried out by traditional broadcasters and production companies. These elements are fundamental in understanding why some products travel well, while others do not, and how come certain markets have more exchange between them or in a mostly unidirectional way, or why do certain types of products become traded in a different way than others.

## The four tenets of cultural transduction

The next step in the development of our common lexicon to talk about cultural transduction was to define the main aspects we could concentrate on when discussing why products are traded, altered and consumed in different markets. We wanted to be able to answer the basic four questions of *where, what, how,* and *by whom* was the cultural transduction carried out (see Table 1.1). The issues highlighted above, led us to think of specific aspects that could be studied when looking at this phenomenon. The first one that came to mind was the markets in which the product had been developed and inserted.

The question here regarded the characteristics of those markets, the likelihood of exchange of products between them; the commonalities or differences they exhibit which may promote or hinder exchanges between them. Undoubtedly, one of the main issues with audiovisual products that came to mind immediately was the language of the product. Countries, regions, or parts of countries that share common languages tend to have audiovisual exchanges. Whether it be major official languages, like German between Austria,

*Table 1.1* The tenets of cultural transduction

| Market | Product | People | Process |
|---|---|---|---|
| The focus is the place where the travel occurs or is intended to happen. The characteristics of the involved markets are studied to understand the likelihood of products travelling between them. | The traits and qualities of a product determine the complexity of travel to a given market. Understanding these traits is key to assess the chances of access to multiple markets. | This tenet engages with the roles and activities carried out by people to find, select, assess, negotiate, and insert products into other markets. Recognising their tastes, values and motivations is key to know how they influence the travels of products. | The institutions or organisations involved have their own structures, activities, interests, and motivations to include cultural or media products from other markets. The way they define and organise their activities are fundamental to understand how they promote or hinder travel. |

Switzerland and Germany, minority languages in one country that might be majority languages in another, as is the case of French in Canada in relation to France, or diaspora communities, Hindi or Urdu speakers who moved from India to the UK, just to mention a few, it is clear that the language used in a product generates – or hinders – opportunities to cross over to other markets. It could also be that a political space levies high taxes to foreign products, motivating more local production, censors some content, or has historic ties with another specific market from which it derives many of their media consumption. All these aspects have a bearing on whether a product from another market can be made available elsewhere. Studying the specificities of each market in relation to another became one of the aspects to focus upon, and thus, became the first tenet to explore (Chapter 2 is dedicated to this debate).

But despite those historical ties, common languages and trading agreements, some products manage to travel into unexpected territories. There is something about specific products that render them more likely to be consumed beyond their originally intended market or the place where they were conceived. Whether it is *Yo soy Betty, la fea* making it all the way to be adapted in Russia and India, to the multiplicity of versions of *Big Brother*, and *Who wants to be a millionaire* (Chalaby, 2012a), the appeal of the film *Avatar* (2010) with indigenous communities all over the world (Mirrlees, 2013) and the recent enjoyment of K-Pop as part of the Korean *Hallyu* wave in Latin America (Arriojas & Réquiz, 2019), there is something that particular products might have that sets them apart from the rest and allows for their consumption in a different setting. Clearly, some of these products undergo some form of modification to suit the local interests and tastes, but other manage to enter markets without major alterations. When Straubhaar (1991) originally spoke about cultural proximity, he had something like this in mind. He referred to how the product, in this case telenovelas, resonated with the audiences in various countries in Latin America. Of course, it could be hinted that similar historical and cultural characteristics of the market, including Spanish as a common language for most of the countries in Latin America, was one of the reasons these products could travel well, but not all products were traded with equal success, providing evidence that some products had specific characteristics that rendered them more likely to travel than others. That is the main concern of the product tenet, through which we explore all the characteristics specific products may have that allow them to travel better than others (Chapter 3 addresses this aspect).

The question then moves on to how these products ended up travelling in the first place. How do people from different markets know that there are these other great products that they would be willing to see, consume, or get their hands on. In fact, since many of the products are changed as they go from one market to the other, there may be many people involved in the selection, acquisition, distribution, and modification of these products. It is not as simple as having a hit in one market for it to make it to another one. Apart from legal jurisdictions, trade barriers and linguistic distance that may be considered under the market tenet, and the possible quality and shareability of a product that would make it desirable, which we would study under the product tenet, people have been involved in deciding which products should aim to travel, and how are they supposed to be incorporated into their new market. Whether it is hit radio shows a travelling salesman enjoyed while abroad, videotapes offered at discount prices in a bazaar of likeminded individuals, or the dedicated efforts of international fans of *manga* to expand the market of their favourite titles, people engage with media products and in their engagement provide ways for them to travel between markets. Cuelenaere (2020) has found this approach to the cultural mediators by the cultural transduction framework as useful because it showcases a "broadly defined typology is that it is easily transposable to other industrial and cultural contexts, which makes it, for instance, highly (but not solely) applicable to the remake industry" (p. 215). Focusing on the people involved in those processes seemed like a very important aspect to understand how the cultural transduction was developed. This became the third aspect to address, known as the people tenet (Chapter 4 is all about this tenet).

Now, if we recognise that most products are altered, even if minimally, when they travel between markets, with some keeping more of their initial characteristics than others, it becomes important to know what processes took place in the alterations experienced by the product. If a comparison of the places of original production and insertion is the concern under the market tenet, the qualities of the individual product are reviewed under the product tenet, and the people involved in the transformation are the concern of the people tenet, the final thing to consider would be the form, procedure or structure through which the processes take place. Formal and informal settings with a variety of regulations, procedures, strategies, and aims underscore why some products travel, while others do not. From Hollywood studios acquiring European films for remakes, to *anime* characters being subtitled in other languages from the comfort of a bedroom for a video website (see Orrego Carmona, 2013; Pérez-González, 2006), to the transformation of the physical distribution in DVD within Nigeria and to neighbouring countries via formal or informal networks into digital platforms (see Lobato, 2010; Ebelebe, 2019), or video games being altered to suit a different console or platform in localisation companies in Thailand (Schleiner, 2020, pp. 144–145), there are varied processes through which these products are presented and accommodated for a different audience (Chapter 5 concentrates on this issue).

Of course, many of these aspects had already been studied from a variety of disciplines and by academics from many departments. But to be able to apply them together for specific cases, or separately by tenet for each aspect, would allow for a more nuanced understanding of how and why cultural products travel the globe.

## Cultural transduction applied

The question about how *Yo soy Betty, la fea* became *Verliebt in Berlin* was not an easy one to solve. That is why I embarked on this quest to create a useful tool to navigate how situations, akin to that one, develop. The cultural transduction framework was the response. It is a structured system based on previous academic work, to provide a simplified and organised language that would help discussing these issues. The four tenets illustrate aspects that can be addressed separately (see Table 1.1) or together. Like any human construct that we create to make sense of the world that surrounds us, it has not been without flaws, and I am indebted to all those who, by trying to apply it in whole or in part to their own research interests, have shown its limitations. The criticism levied has been fundamental to improve the model and to refine it.

The critique brought forth by Cattrysse (2017), regarding how the debates of cultural transduction resounded with work previously done in adaptation studies, made perfect sense. The original idea of studying the phenomena under cultural transduction had come from television studies grounded in political economy, rather than in literature or film studies. Certainly, there has been more focus in elements from adaptation studies in latter usage of the cultural transduction framework, and they have been central to its development. But Cattrysse also praised the multidisciplinary approach of the framework, something that it has also been able to attain thanks to the application by academics from various disciplines. Thus, cultural transduction seems to respond to the observation that "one of the main reasons that theories fail adaptation studies is that most stem from single disciplines and are therefore inadequate to address intermedial operations" (Elliot, 2013, p. 36). In the following chapters, more detailed application and criticism is made based on specific tenets, with the hope that this framework continues to be improved and strengthened.

The framework has also expanded to cover more than just television shows and includes other forms of media and cultural production, such as video games, memes and film. The aim for this framework is to be applied beyond each single medium and maybe even to become useful as a set of guidelines for those interested in developing their own travelling products (see Chapter 6 for a set of useful guidelines). The framework would benefit the more it is put to the test and other perspectives are brought into account. That is one of the main goals of this book, to expand the reach of the framework, invite criticism to help improve it for future studies and applications.

## Note

1 A language is defined more by politics than by linguistics. When a language is considered discrete and distinct from others it is given a name, which sometimes includes and sometimes excludes elements that are found in the way the users of the language often use to communicate. Named languages tend to have institutions that

define their boundaries and keep control of how they are used, what is considered
to be an appropriate use of the language and what would be considered incorrect,
providing a normative description of the language (see Otheguy et al., 2015; Eberhard et al., 2023, "Methodology"). Sometimes the variation within named languages
is considerable and translators often specify the version of the language used (e.g.
Portuguese between Brazil and Portugal).

# References

Arriojas, D., & Réquiz, I. V. (2019). Devorando el Hallyu: Desarrollo, hibridación y
canibalismo latinoamericano [Devouring the Hallyu: Development, hybridization,
and Latin American cannibalism]. *Revista Mundo Asia Pacífico, 8*(14), 45–59.
https://doi.org/10.17230/map.v8.i14.03
Cambridge Dictionary. (2023). Transduction. https://dictionary.cambridge.org/
dictionary/english/transduction?q=Transduction
Cattrysse, P. (2017). Cultural transduction and adaptation studies: The concept of
cultural proximity. *Palabra Clave, 20*(3), 645–662. https://doi.org/10.5294/pacla.
2017.20.3.3
Chalaby, J. K. (2011). The making of an entertainment revolution: How the TV format
trade became a global industry. *European Journal of Communication, 26*(4), 293–309.
https://doi.org/10.1177/0267323111423414
Chalaby, J. K. (2012a). At the origin of a global industry: The TV format trade as an
Anglo-American invention. *Media, Culture & Society, 34*(1), 36–52. https://doi.
org/10.1177/0163443711427198
Chalaby, J. K. (2012b). Producing Tv Content in a globalized intellectual property market: The emergence of the international production model. *Journal of Media Business Studies, 9*(3), 19–39. https://doi.org/10.1080/16522354.2012.11073550
Chalaby, J. K. (2015). The advent of the transnational TV format trading system: a
global commodity chain analysis. *Media, Culture & Society, 37*(3), 460–478. https://
doi.org/10.1177/0163443714567017
Chalaby, J. K. (2016). Drama without drama: The late rise of scripted TV formats.
*Television & New Media, 17*(1), 3–20. https://doi.org/10.1177/1527476414561089
Conway, K. (2012a). A conceptual and empirical approach to cultural translation.
*Translation Studies, 5*(3), 264–279. https://doi.org/10.1080/14781700.2012.701938
Conway, K. (2012b). Cultural translation, global television studies, and the circulation
of telenovelas in the United States. *International Journal of Cultural Studies, 15*(6),
583–598. https://doi.org/10.1177/1367877911422291
Conway, K. (2020). *The art of cummunication in a polarized World.* AU Press.
Cuelenaere, E. (2020). Towards an integrative methodological approach of film re-
make studies. *Adaptation, 13*(2), 210–223. https://doi.org/10.1093/ADAPTATION/
APZ033
Dorfman, A., & Mattelart, A. (1998). *Para Leer al Pato Donald: Comunicación de
Masa y Colonialismo.* Siglo XXI Editores.
Ebelebe, U. B. (2019). Reinventing Nollywood: The impact of online funding and
distribution on Nigerian cinema. *Convergence, 25*(3), 466–478. https://doi.org/
10.1177/1354856517735792

Eberhard, D. M., Simons, G. F., and Fennig, C. D. (eds.). (2023). *Ethnologue: Languages of the world*. SIL International. Online version: http://www.ethnologue.com.

Elleström, L. (2017). Adaptations as intermediality. In T. Leitch (Ed.), *The Oxford handbook of adaptation studies* (pp. 509–526). Oxford University Press.

Elliott, K. (2013). Theorizing adaptations/adapting theories. In J. Bruhn, A. Gjelsvik, & E. F. Hanssen (Eds.), *Adaptation studies: New challenges, new directions* (pp. 19–46). Bloomsbury.

Engelstad, A. (2018). Playing the producer's game: Adaptation and the question of fidelity. *Adaptation, 11*(1), 25–39. https://doi.org/10.1093/adaptation/apx023

Esser, A. (2013a). TV formats: History, theory, industry and audiences. *Critical Studies in Television, 8*(2), vii–xvi. https://doi.org/10.7227/CST.8.2.1

Esser, A. (2013b). The format business: Franchising television content. *International Journal of Digital Television, 4*(2), 141–158. https://doi.org/10.1386/jdtv.4.2.141_1

Esser, A. (2010). Television formats: Primetime staple, global market. *Popular Communication, 8*(4), 273–292. https://doi.org/10.1080/15405702.2010.514176

Hermansson, C. (2015). Flogging fidelity: In defense of the (un)dead horse. *Adaptation, 8*(2), 147–160. https://doi.org/10.1093/adaptation/apv014

Hutcheon, L. (2013). *A theory of adaptation*. Routledge.

La Pastina, A. C., & Straubhaar, J. D. (2005). Multiple proximities between television genres and audiences: The schism between telenovelas' global distribution and local consumption. *International Communication Gazette, 67*(3), 271–288. https://doi.org/10.1177/0016549205052231

Lobato, R. (2010). Creative industries and informal economies: Lessons from Nollywood. *International Journal of Cultural Studies, 13*(4), 337–354. https://doi.org/10.1177/1367877910369971

López Charles, C. (2008). Transduction between image and sound in compositional processes. *Perception, 485*, 1–5.

Maitland, S. (2017). *What is cultural translation?* Bloomsbury.

Martín Barbero, J. (1987). *De los medios a las mediaciones. Comunicación, cultura y hegemonía*. G. Gili.

Martín Barbero, J. (2005). Memory and form in the Latin American soap opera. In R. Allen, (ed.), *To be continued: Soap operas around the world* (pp. 276–284). Routledge.

Mato, D. (2005). The Transnationalization of the telenovela industry, territorial references, and the production of markets and representations of transnational identities. *Television & New Media, 6*(4), 423–444. https://doi.org/10.1177/1527476403255822

Miller, J. L. (2010). Ugly Betty goes global: Global networks of localized content in the telenovela industry. *Global Media and Communication, 6*(2), 198–217. https://doi.org/10.1177/1742766510373717

Moran, A. (2004). Television formats in the world/the world of television formats. In A. Moran & M. Keane (Eds.), *Television across Asia: Television industries, programme formats and globalization* (pp. 1–8). Routledge.

Moran, A. (2009). *New flows in global TV*. Intellect.

Moran, A. (2013). Global television formats: Genesis and growth. *Critical Studies in Television: The International Journal of Television Studies, 8*(2), 1–19. https://doi.org/10.7227/CST.8.2.2

14    *What is cultural transduction?*

Moran, A., & Aveyard, K. (2014). The place of television programme formats. *Journal of Media and Cultural Studies, 28*(1), 18–27. Https://doi.org/10.1080/10304312.2014.870869

Murray, S. (2012). *The adaptation industry: The cultural economy of contemporary literary adaptation.* Routledge.

Murray, S. (2008). Materializing adaptation theory: The adaptation industry. *Literature/Film Quarterly, 36*(1), 4–20.

Otheguy, R., García, O., & Reid, W. (2015). Clarifying translanguaging and deconstructing named languages: A perspective from linguistics. *Applied Linguistics Review, 6*(3), 281–307. https://doi.org/10.1515/applirev-2015-0014

Orrego Carmona, D. (2013). Avance de la traducción audiovisual: desde los inicios hasta la era digital. *Mutatis Mutandis, 6*(2), 297–320.

Pérez-González, L. (2006). Fansubbing Anime: Insights into the "butterfly effect" of globalization in audiovisual translation. *Perspectives: Studies in Translatology, 14*(4), 260–277.

Rivera-Betancur, J. L., & Uribe-Jongbloed, E. (2012). La Suerte de la Fea, muchas la desean: de Yo soy Betty, la Fea a Ugly Betty. In M. Pérez (Ed.), *Previously on* (pp. 825–842). Universidad de Salamanca.

Schleiner, A.-M. (2020). *Transnational play.* Amsterdam University Press.

Sherry, J. (2016). Adaptation studies through screenwriting studies: Transitionality and the adapted screenplay. *Journal of Screenwriting, 7*(1), 11–28. https://doi.org/10.1386/josc.7.1.11

Straubhaar, J. D. (1991). Beyond media imperialism: Assymetrical interdependence and cultural proximity. *Critical Studies in Mass Comunication, 8*(1), 39–59.

Straubhaar, J. D. (2007). *World television: From global to local.* Sage Publications.

Straubhaar, J. D. (2021). Cultural proximity. In D.Y. Jin (ed.), *The Routledge handbook of digital media and globalization* (pp. 24–33). Routledge.

Szwydky, L. L. (2023). CODA: Transmedia cultural history, convergence culture and the future of adaptation studies. In L.L. Szwydky & G. Jellenik (Eds.), *Adaptation before cinema: Literary and visual convergence from antiquity through the nineteenth century* (pp. 283–303). PalgraveMacmillan. https://doi.org/10.1007/978-3-031-09596-2_13

Tunstall, J. (1977). *The media are American.* Sage.

Uribe-Jongbloed, E., & Espinosa-Medina, H. D. (2014). A clearer picture: Towards a new framework for the study of cultural transduction in audiovisual market trades. *Observatorio, 8*(1), 23–48.

# 2 The market tenet

## The ebbs and flows of cultural and media trade between markets

Cultural products do not flow freely the world over. Some products reach us while others do not. Whether it is a film, a TV show, a song, a painting, a video games, or a comic book, there are products that can be found in many different places in the world, while some others never seem to pop up. The reason why some of the products might be available beyond the places where they were created depends on a great variety of factors, some of them as simple as political borders or as complex as one-to-one negotiations based on real or perceived local tastes.

One way to try to disentangle why some products travel while others do not is to take a look at the particular markets in which those products came to being and in those others where they may or may not be found. The easiest image that comes to mind when thinking about these issues is the border and customs controls at airports and land crossings. One common idea is that the political construct we call a nation is, at once, a market. Thus, we think of markets in a national scale, and we consider how cultural goods cross over from one place to another, by imagining they cross a given national border, where agents in charge of border and customs control decide whether a product can cross into the other nation or not. Much like the passport control officer in the video game *Papers, please!* (Pope, 2013), the decision of individuals based on legislative and trade regulations at those borders, define whether products go through or not. National markets are relevant, because they tend to be regulated under one general legislation that applies, more or less equally and homogenously over the whole territory. They are usually also the entities that collect data, so national markets are easy to map out based on borders, data and political structure, and despite supranational institutions like the World Trade Organisation or UNESCO and globalisation processes, Nation-States remain the central sites in charge of exercising control upon citizens and institutions, particularly with regards to the media (Flew & Waisbord, 2015).

However, there are other ways in which markets operate that might be either supranational (think or the European Union or Mercosur) or intranational, as is the case of particular political entities within countries with specific control over certain cultural goods including television broadcast, as

DOI: 10.4324/9781003380221-2

is the case of the Province of Quebec, the Basque Country, Wales, or Hong Kong, within the States they are part of. Markets, then, are defined also by other forms of political structures that allow or constrain the transfer of certain products. Nowadays, companies expand over various Nation-States and might define markets according rather to their presence or absence in given territories, more so than national borders. And with the advent of truly international interconnections available through the internet, there might even be transnational markets in virtual spaces, where some forms of trade may take place. Thus, the main aspect is "to go beyond framing the debate in terms of 'the passing' or 'the persistence' of the state and instead understand how local, national, and global forces shape media politics and policies" (Flew & Waisbord, 2015, p. 632).

Access to markets then depends on the interplay of regulations, boundaries, and limitations. They may manifest in trade barriers, censorship, or embargoes that impede the entry of certain products or they may shape up to be defined under local interests, tastes, or preferences that discourage the insertion of some products while privileging others. Historical connections, trading patterns, colonial legacies – oftentimes hand in hand with linguistic normalisation – are also reasons that have made some markets approach one another while avoiding others, even similar ones.

One way to explore how and why some products make it through to other markets is to look at how these different barriers, borders, and limits are set up, in relation to a given point of departure. What are the characteristics shared between one market and another one, that may explain why movies from certain countries are watched while others are not, whose TV dramas you present dubbed or with audio commentary, which ones do you adapt locally or why are others copied without shame. Let's look at all these aspects related to the market.

## Barriers between markets

Each market, whether national, regional, or supranational, has certain entry requirements for cultural products coming from abroad. In some cases, they might include limits or quotas regarding how many products from a different setting may enter the market in relation to local production. Requirements of this ilk might include an interest in promoting local production, defend cultural interests, or prevent the flooding of products from other markets that produce more content, as a way to prevent job losses in the local market or to fence off fears of cultural assimilation. From total ban to limited quotas, or from import taxes to access to local subsidies, each cultural market provides different types of entry barriers reliant on regulation or political control of cultural production (for film trade barriers, see Marvasti & Canterbery, 2005). Apart from those which are consigned in different forms of legislation, other barriers might be part of how people have been used to trade certain products, and the demands in those areas are less clear, although commonly shared. They include a reluctance or opposition to certain type of content or to specific products which might include accepted mythologies about what kind of content a local market may not be willing to accept (see Carlson & Corliss, 2011 for the case of video games). Although this might boil down to specific individuals (as will be covered in Chapter 4), it becomes translated into certain forms of secondary regulation, or rating boards (Driscoll & Grealy, 2019) for products, including films (see Pett, 2014) and video games (see Carlson & Corliss, 2011, pp. 66–67).

One way of looking at these restrictions could be by assessing them against one another and creating an index of openness or closeness of each market. This is what Nordås et al. (2014) did to measure the restrictiveness of national markets in regard to audiovisual services. What they provide is a Services Trade Restrictiveness Index that signals how countries could be measured in terms of the accessibility or restrictiveness of their markets. This would be useful when assessing the way products travel between markets. As presented in their conclusions, there are more restrictions for audiovisual broadcast media than for films, although films are also more restricted in their flow than sound recordings. It would seem to align with ideas about quotas on foreign content in the case of television broadcast and, although in a reduced manner, in cinema exhibition. These barriers are also changing constantly, in an ebb and flow of measures that respond to the perceived cultural risks. For instance, in Asia rather than strong national barriers, there seems to exist a relatively lower control nowadays, because

> whereas a profound cultural anxiety coupled with a desire to safeguard the integrity of closed national spaces from external influences clearly dominated early responses to media globalization, the region's current media discourse represents a decisive pivoting away from this position
>
> (Chadha & Kavoori, 2015, p. 486).

However, despite the barriers, cultural products flow constantly in a globalised market. The omnipresence of Hollywood films, Japanese *anime* and English-language rock seem to highlight that the flow of cultural products is not even the world over, but examples such as Turkish telenovelas in Latin America and K-Pop concerts all over Asia exemplify that there are other simultaneous flows taking place in the world.

## On the flows of global products

There has been a consistent debate about the direction of flow of cultural products which has been addressed by academia and international agencies. Perhaps the best reminder of this debate was the 1980 UNESCO "one world, many voices" document known as the McBride report after the chairman of the committee in charge of producing it. The report claimed for a more balanced production and circulation of news and other cultural products, but its recommendations were disregarded in favour of liberalisation of markets and conglomeration of media corporations (Krakowiak & Mastrini, 2019, p. 43). Debates about a single directional flow of cultural goods from developed nations, mainly the US and Western Europe, although also from the Soviet bloc, was soon displaced by new theories of asymmetrical interdependence or contraflows (for instance, Straubhaar, 1991; Iwabuchi, 2000; Thussu, 2007), that highlighted other international exchanges taking place in regions throughout the world.

Under a similar perspective as Straubhaar (1991), Thussu (2007) offers a model that recognises a central or core market generating a great amount of cultural content to other markets and defining it as the dominant flow, while also acknowledging there are other flows either regional or aimed at diaspora communities, which he sets under the term contra-flows. Through this explanation he signals that

> Though the Northern conglomerates continue to shape the global media landscape, the flow of global media products is not just one way from the media-rich North (and within it the Anglo-American axis) to the media-poor South. There is evidence that in an increasingly global communication environment, new transnational networks have emerged, including from the periphery to the metropolitan centres of global media.
>
> (Thussu, 2007, p. 2).

This further expansion led Uribe-Jongbloed and Espinosa-Medina (2014) to provide a new structure that tried to place these different types of flow between core and peripheral markets. In it they set North America, Western Europe, and Japan as core markets, while all others could be considered peripheral, in terms of cultural production, particularly audiovisual media. Despite the existence of those contra-flows within or beyond the peripheral markets, "developed countries still dominate the flows of cultural services worldwide. From 2006 to 2018, little to no improvement was recorded for cultural services from developing countries entering the global market" (Deloumeaux, 2022, p. 181).

Mirrlees (2013) has shown how the debate on the flows of entertainment media can be placed between two camps, those presenting the scene as Cultural Imperialism (CI), through which the economical and media powerful countries dominate and try to homogenise the world, and those embracing a Cultural Globalisation (CG) paradigm that see the interaction and expansion of global entertainment media as culturally and socially positive. Although his in-depth analysis between those two camps is beyond the scope of this text, he offers a way out of having to choose between these positions, when he claims that a challenge for twenty-first century global media studies may be the development of a middle ground paradigm that does not tirelessly or naively defend the supposed claims to truth of the CI paradigm or the CG paradigm. Too often, these two paradigms appear in literature reviews and skirmishes between ideologues on the Left and Right as caricatures or straw men, when the research associated with each paradigm is often more supple, complex, and nuanced.

(Mirrlees, 2013, p. 57)

For instance, from the perspective of the trade of TV formats, there is something to be said about it starting as an Anglo-American invention flowing mostly from Europe by the end of the 20th century (Chalaby, 2012), but recognising also that second-tier or mid-range audiovisual production nations, for instance Colombia and Argentina in Latin America (Uribe-Jongbloed & Pis-Diez, 2017) or South Korea in Asia (UNCTAD, 2010, p. 1; Straubhaar, 2007, p. 6), have achieved considerable notoriety in those flows. It remains as curious that although the production location of contemporary cinema has moved to various nations, the main decisions and capital concentration remain within the confines of Hollywood (Miller et al., 2005). So, although many countries can now boast that they are the filming locations of great Hollywood movies, the central capital and cultural decisions of their products remain anchored in the same core market they have always been found.

Even if the new digital expansion has been hailed as the clearest evidence of globalised interconnectedness, that would render the idea of differential and distant markets as a memory of old, "the global digital market is far from united and that national borders, center-periphery hierarchies and differences in scale still matter, and perhaps they matter even more than in the analog broadcast era" (Szczepanik et al., 2020, p. 1). Thus, for the interest of cultural transduction, understanding the positioning of markets in relation to one another remains central to understanding how cultural products travel.

## Cultural proximity, discount and distance

In the developing of his description of asymmetrical interdependence, Straubhaar (1991) coined the concept of cultural proximity to describe the characteristics that were shared between products from one market and a receiving audience in another. In further work he would expand the characteristics that make up what he considers to be part of the cultural proximity, mentioning that

> most audiences seem to prefer television programs that are as close to
> them as possible in language, ethnic appearance, dress, style, humor, historical reference, and shared topical knowledge. This is not necessarily a
> national phenomenon. Audiences can be attracted or feel proximities to

local culture, regional cultures within their nation, national culture, and transnational cultural regions or spaces.

(Straubhaar, 2007, p. 26)

As Straubhaar (2007) implies, cultural proximity is not connected exclusively to a national identity but other forms of identity that may align, as well, with other markets (i.e. regional, linguistic, or supranational). In his recap of the concept, Straubhaar (2021) points out that cultural and linguistic capital have a bearing upon media consumption choices, with wealth acquisition underlying the increase in choice and a possible challenge to local consumption, leading to more cosmopolitan tastes.

An issue that is not immediately clear, is if cultural proximity applies between any specific given product and an audience (see, for instance, Castelló, 2010), or if it could be used to signal the potential commonalities of two or more markets. Straubhaar (2007, 2021) tends to refer to both instances when he uses cultural proximity. However, cultural proximity between a product and an audience may respond to existent cultural proximity between the producing and receiving markets. That is the interpretation that Moran and Keane (2004) have made of the concept when they state that "the high degree of cultural proximity between Taiwan and South Korea means that the narratives of Korean dramas also reflect life in Taiwan" (pp. 58–59). Since the characteristics that would make a product interesting or understandable for another market might include elements beyond cultural commonality (see Chapter 3), it seems more appropriate to restrict cultural proximity as a characteristic to observe between markets, as per the interpretation of Moran and Keane, when taken as a part of the cultural transduction framework.

Another concept closely related to cultural proximity is cultural discount. Cultural discount refers to the loss of value or interest for products stemming from markets with low cultural proximity to the target market (Lee, 2006; McFadyen et al., 2000, p. 2; Hoskins & Mirrus, 1988). The cultural discount is then applied to each product when they try to gain access to a less proximate market. What this entails is that

this cultural discount vis-à-vis domestic art limits the degree of trade: the closer (national) cultures are, the smaller the difference in the relevant consumption capital and, thus, the larger the bilateral trade in art. This cultural discount can be asymmetric; one country can accumulate consumption capital for the other country's culture, but the opposite need not be true.

(Schulze, 2003, p. 270)

Schulze's (2003) explanations clarify why there is very little cultural discount between certain markets of ample cultural distance, because people have been previously exposed to sufficient cultural elements from another market to understand its products, but it does not imply that it also applies the other way around. US cultural products have reached many markets and that has made them less prone to cultural discount than products flowing from those markets into the US. When defining cultural proximity, it is also important to understand how it correlates to cultural discount and, thus, how it limits the way in which predictability for the success of one cultural product could be based on its success in a different market.

## Cross-cultural predictability and cultural tolerance

Similarity in cultural traits between markets allows for assumptions about the success that particular products would have when exchanged between markets. This is the premise of cross-cultural predictability. To test it, Lee (2006) looked at the box office results of movies in the US and Hong Kong, and tried to see which movies exhibited the best predictability between the markets. The results show that comedies have high cultural discount and low cross-culture predictability – as one would expect for the low cultural proximity between the US and Hong Kong, whereas science-fiction films presented lower cultural discount and the box office results were more predictable. The idea, then, that cultural proximity could serve to account for cross-cultural predictability appears to prove only partially true, because the difference between the results according to film genre highlights that there are specificities of the product that have a bearing when they are to be consumed elsewhere.

Similarly, Fu (2012) has shown that both language and culture are fundamental to determine film consumption and genre acceptance, based on box-office results for major US films in other markets, pointing out that

> differences in culture can be strategically tempered by program or marketing design, but language diversity is more difficult to deal with simply because there is no way for a foreign audience to be attracted to a movie if they cannot follow the dialogue.
>
> (p. 810)

Thus, although both cultural and linguistic proximity are fundamental, providing further support to cross-cultural predictability, language comes as a better predictor than culture in general, supporting the relevance of thinking about geolinguistic regions (Sinclair, 2000), and reglocalisation strategies (Piñon, 2014), that look at how to reach regional markets that share linguistic traits.

The trade in television formats has often been predicated upon cross-cultural predictability, because of "the higher probability of success (risk reduction) based on the assumption that success in one market is an indicator for success in a foreign market" (Lantzsch et al., 2009, p. 81). It was the success of *Yo soy Betty, la fea* in Colombia which prompted the interests to buy it as a finished product or, later, as a format in many countries the world over. Cross-cultural predictability remains important today for all sorts of media products, including video games and mobile apps (see Shaheer et al., 2020).

Another element that could be discussed here would be the openness of certain markets to products from a different one. This idea of cultural tolerance includes the disposition to receive production that may be developed elsewhere, to assume that it is acceptable to a given market. For instance, in China "games are classified as cultural products, and are subject to vigorous scrutinization by state censors. Entry into the Chinese market is also dictated by stringent stipulations ranging from story lines and graphic content to venue of publishing and distribution" (Tai & Lu, 2021, p. 213), which means that there is low cultural tolerance and requires for foreign video game producers to include local partners to overcome cultural and market barriers.

Cultural tolerance might include alliances based on political or historical agreements, such as the EU media production and distribution agreements, associations made between countries which share linguistic links, and other international treaties based on colonial history, but may also relate to direct efforts of soft-power undertaken by large producers of content. That was the case of the US bundling strategies in the 1950s–1970s, Mexican telenovelas and Japanese *animes* had similar strategies in the 1970–1980s in Latin America and also the recent incursion of drama production from China in large parts of Africa (Lei, 2019). In fact, the streamers' strategies with their catalogue of reruns might be a new form of bundling (Gilbert, 2019). By flooding markets with their production usually for free or with very low entry prices, other markets become used to otherwise culturally distant products. The rise of the audiovisual distribution giant Netflix (see Box 2.1) and other streamers has provided new pathways to bridge conventional market entries and distributions, challenging some of the established cultural tolerance barriers and providing new protectionist debates around cultural production in various parts of the world, as well as presenting new opportunities to discuss definitions of audiovisual products that may qualify for local tax rebates and other incentives (see the case of *Narcos* in Uribe-Jongbloed et al., 2021, p. 75).

## The relevance of studying markets

Products travel between different markets based on a variety of reasons, and knowing some of the nuances of the processes that take place between different levels and locations of markets is central to understand how products travel. Linguistic markets may be very large geo-linguistic regions, as in the case of Spanish-speaking countries (see Sinclair, 2014) including part of the US market (Uribe-Jongbloed & Pis Diez, 2017), but some others might be smaller in size and include a national, regional, or local reach, as in the case of Welsh-language broadcasting within the UK (McElroy et al., 2019), transnational Korean pop music (Ju & Lee, 2015), diaspora and regional consumption of satellite television (Amezaga Albizu, 2007; Chadha & Kavoori, 2015),

## Box 2.1 Netflix and distribution markets

Netflix has become a household name for internet-distributed television in the second decade of the 21st century. Considerable attention has been given to Netflix recently in academia for the changes that its streaming catalogue has brought to various parts of the globe and to the practice of television consumption.

From defining Netflix as the IV age of television (Jenner, 2016), to presenting it as central to new forms of media production, practice, distribution and regulation, Netflix has served as a case in point to study a variety of aspects of transnational audiovisual markets, leading also to updates in international standards for judging what a film actually is, as in the case of the Academy Awards in the US or local definitions of television shows to qualify for local tax rebates. At the centre of contemporary debates on transnational distribution of audiovisual products, markets, policies, and cultural protectionism, Netflix has become the most renowned case to explore difference across the world. The various responses of national and international markets to the advance of internet audiovisual distribution has brought some long-standing debates back to the fore, including the cultural imperialism and protectionism discussions that had been advanced before during the expansion of television canned products, satellite distribution, cable subscription, and, now, digital ubiquitous consumption.

Some fundamental texts on this debate include:

Caminos, A., Médola, A. S. & Suing, A. (Orgs.). (2019). *A Nova Televisão – do Youtube ao Netflix*. Ria Editorial.

Jenner, M. (2018). *Netflix and the re-invention of television*. Springer International Publishing. https://doi.org/10.1007/978-3-319-94316-9

Lobato, R. (2019). *Netflix nations*. New York University Press.

McDonald, K., & Smith-Rowsey, D. (Eds.) (2016). *The Netflix effect*. Bloomsbury Academic.

Orozco, G. (Coord.) (2020). *Televisión en tiempos de Netflix*. Universidad de Guadalajara.

Shattuc, J. (2020). Netflix, Inc., and online television. In J. Wasko & E. R. Meehan (Eds.), *A companion to television* (pp. 145–164). Willey Blackwell.

Straubhaar, J., Santillana, M., de Macedo Higgins Joyce, V., & Duarte, L. G. (2021). *From Telenovelas to Netflix: Transnational, transverse television in Latin America*. Springer International Publishing. https://doi.org/10.1007/978-3-030-77470-7

or the supposed ubiquitous presence of Netflix (Stewart, 2016) and online games (Schleiner, 2020). Examining markets implies dissecting through different forms in which markets are constructed according to language, political control, existing treaties, cultural worries, and emerging sites of production.

The relevance for markets on a national level cannot be underestimated despite globalisation practices because of the continuation of the Nation-State as the main element of regulation and control (Flew & Waisbord, 2015), but it is not the only scenario in which markets may be analysed. Bicket (2005) considered the linguistic aspect as central for studying how certain markets behave through time in relation to one another, to see if they were getting closer or more distant, comparing Quebec-France with English-speaking Canada and the US. Others have insisted that it is key to look at the nuances of small markets (Szczepanik et al., 2020). The importance here lies in the way "research that considers the cultural complexities of audio-visual flows, without diminishing the attention given to imbalances in commercial power and the dynamic nature of ideology would further strengthen the field of flows studies" (Iordache et al., 2018, p. 762).

The main takeaway here is that the market relationship, between where a product stems from and where it is consumed or expected to be inserted into, needs to be explored to evaluate the entry difficulty and the likelihood of success. In those cases where cultural distance would seem ample, other strategies need to be executed to assure entrance. Sometimes the limitation or potential is due to the qualities of specific products (see Chapter 3), the intentions of individuals (see Chapter 4) or the motivations of institutions (see Chapter 5). Now that the study of markets and their characteristics has been presented as one of the ways in which we can understand processes of cultural transduction, we can move to the specificities of given products that might explain or clarify why some of those products travel while others do not.

## References

Amezaga Albizu, J. (2007). Geolinguistic regions and diasporas in the age of satellite television. *International Communication Gazette, 69*(3), 239–261. https://doi.org/10.1177/1748048507076578

Bicket, D. (2005). Reconsidering geocultural contraflow: Intercultural information flows through trends in global audiovisual trade. *Global Media Journal, 4*(6), 1–16.

Carlson, R., & Corliss, J. (2011). Imagined commodities: Video game localization and mythologies of cultural difference. *Games and Culture, 6*(1), 61–82. https://doi.org/10.1177/1555412010377322

Castelló, E. (2010). Dramatizing proximity: Cultural and social discourses in soap operas from production to reception. *European Journal of Cultural Studies, 13*(2), 207–223. https://doi.org/10.1177/1367549409352274

Chadha, K., & Kavoori, A. (2015). The new normal: From media imperialism to market liberalization – Asia's shifting television landscapes. *Media, Culture and Society, 37*(3), 479–492. https://doi.org/10.1177/0163443715574478

Deloumeaux, L. (2022). Global flows of cultural goods and services: Still a one-way trade. In *Re-shaping policies for creativity: addressing culture as a global public good* (pp. 163–181). Unesco. https://unesdoc.unesco.org/ark:/48223/pf0000380474.locale=en

Driscoll, C., & Grealy, L. (2019). In the name of the nation: Media classification, globalisation, and exceptionalism. *International Journal of Cultural Studies, 22*(3), 383–399. https://doi.org/10.1177/1367877918784606

Flew, T., & Waisbord, S. (2015). The ongoing significance of national media systems in the context of media globalization. *Media, Culture & Society, 37*(4), 620–636. https://doi.org/10.1177/0163443714566903

Fu, W. W. (2012). National audience tastes in Hollywood film genres: Cultural distance and linguistic affinity. *Communication Research, 40*(6), 789–817. https://doi.org/10.1177/0093650212442085

Gilbert, A. (2019). Push, pull, rerun: Television reruns and streaming media. *Television and New Media, 20*(7), 686–701. https://doi.org/10.1177/1527476419842418

Hoskins, C., & Mirus, R. (1988). Reasons for the US dominance of the international trade in television programmes. *Media, Culture & Society, 10*(4), 499–504. https://doi.org/10.1177/016344388010004006

Iordache, C., Van Audenhove, L., & Loisen, J. (2019). Global media flows: A qualitative review of research methods in audio-visual flow studies. *International Communication Gazette, 81*(6–8), 748–767. https://doi.org/10.1177/1748048518808650

Iwabuchi, K. (2000). To globalize, regionalize, or localize us, that is the question: Japan's response to media globalization. In G. Wang, J. Servaes, & A. Goonasekera (Eds.), *The new communication landscape: Demystifying media globalization* (pp. 142–59). Routledge.

Jenner, M. (2016). Is this TVIV? On Netflix, TVIII and binge-watching. *New Media and Society, 18*(2), 257–273. https://doi.org/10.1177/1461444814541523

Ju, H., & Lee, S. (2015). The Korean wave and Asian Americans: The ethnic meanings of transnational Korean pop culture in the USA. *Continuum, 29*(3), 1–16. https://doi.org/10.1080/10304312.2014.986059

Krakowiak, F. & Mastrini, G. (2019). Flujos audiovisuales en América Latina. Enseñanzas y desafíos. *Chasqui, 142,* 37–56.

Lantzsch, K., Altmeppen, K.-D., & Will, A. (2009). Trading in TV entertainment: An analysis. In A. Moran (Ed.), *TV formats worldwide. Localizing global programs* (pp. 77–96). Intellect.

Lee, F. L. F. (2006). Cultural discount and cross-culture predictability: Examining the box office performance of American movies in Hong Kong. *Journal of Media Economics, 19*(4), 259–278. https://doi.org/10.1207/s15327736me1904_3

Lei, W. (2019). Encountering Chinese modernity: The emerging popularity of Chinese television drama in East Africa. *Wiener Zeitschrift für kritische Afrikastudien/Vienna Journal of African Studies, 19*(36), 27–49. https://doi.org/10.25365/phaidra.256_03

Marvasti, A., & Canterbery, E. R. (2005). Cultural and other barriers to motion pictures trade. *Economic Inquiry, 43*(1), 39–54. https://doi.org/10.1093/ei/cbi004

McElroy, R., Papagiannouli, C., & Wiliam, H. (2019). Broadcasting after devolution: Policy and critique in the Welsh media landscape 2008–2015. *International Journal of Cultural Policy, 25*(3), 377–391. https://doi.org/10.1080/10286632.2016.1268133

McFadyen, S., Hoskins, C., & Finn, A. (2000). Cultural industries from an economic/business research perspective. *Canadian Journal of Communication, 25*(1), 1–11. http://cjc-online.ca/index.php/journal/article/view/1146/1065

Miller, T., Govil, N., McMurria, J., Maxwell, R., & Wang, T. (2005). *Global Hollywood 2*. BFI.

Mirrlees, T. (2013). *Global entertainment media. Between cultural imperialism and cultural globalization*. Routledge.

Moran, A., & Keane, M. (2004). *Television across Asia: Television industries, programme formats and globalization*. Routledge.

Nordås, H. K., Lejárraga, I., Miroudot, S., Gonzales, F., Grosso, M. G., Rouzet, D., & Ueno, A. (2014). Services trade restrictiveness index (STRI): Audio-visual services. *OECD Trade Policy Papers, 174*, 1–38. https://doi.org/10.1787/5jxt4nj4fc22-en

Pett, E. (2015) A new media landscape? The BBFC, extreme cinema as cult, and technological change. *New Review of Film and Television Studies, 13*:1, 83–99, https://doi.org/10.1080/17400309.2014.982910

Piñón, J. (2014). Reglocalization and the rise of the network cities media system in producing telenovelas for hemispheric audiences. *International Journal of Cultural Studies, 17*(6), 655–671. https://doi.org/10.1177/1367877913515867

Schleiner, A.-M. (2020). Introduction: Transnational play. In *Transnational play: Piracy, urban art, and mobile games* (pp. 7–26). Amsterdam University Press. Https://doi.org/10.5117/9789463728904_intro

Schulze, G. G. (2003). International trade. In R. Towse (Ed.), *A handbook of cultural economics* (pp. 269–275). Edward Elgar Publishing Limited.

Shaheer, N., Li, S., & Priem, R. (2020). Revisiting location in a digital age: How can lead markets accelerate the internationalization of mobile apps? *Journal of International Marketing, 28*(4), 21–40. https://doi.org/10.1177/1069031X20949457

Sinclair, J. (2014). Transnationalisation of television programming in the Iberoamerican region. *MATRIZes, 8*(2), 63–77. https://doi.org/10.11606/issn.1982-8160.v8i2p63-77

Sinclair, J. (2000). Geolinguistic region as global space: The case of Latin America. In G. Wang, J. Servaes, & A. Goonasekera (Eds.), *The new communications landscape* (pp. 19–32). Routledge.

Stewart, M. (2016). The myth of televisual ubiquity. *Television & New Media, 17*(8), 691–705. https://doi.org/10.1177/1527476416655384

Straubhaar, J. D. (2021). Cultural proximity. In D.Y. Jin (Ed.), *The Routledge handbook of digital media and globalization* (pp. 24–33). Routledge.

Straubhaar, J. D. (1991). Beyond media imperialism: Assymetrical interdependence and cultural proximity. *Critical Studies in Mass Comunication, 8*(1), 39–59.

Szczepanik, P., Zahrádka, P. & Macek, J. (2020). Introduction: Theorizing digital peripheries. In P. Szczepanik, P. Zahrádka, J. Macke & P. Stepan (Eds.), *Digital peripheries: the online circulation of audiovisual content from the small market perspective* (pp. 1–31). Springer.

Tai, Z. & Lu, J. (2021). Playing with Chinese characteristics: The landscape of video games in China. In D.Y. Jin (Ed.), *The Routledge handbook of digital media and globalization* (pp. 206–214). Routledge.

Thussu, D. K. (2007). Mapping global media flow and contra-flow. In D. K. Thussu (Ed.), *Media on the move: Global flow and contra-flow* (pp. 221–238). Routledge.

Uribe-Jongbloed, E., Gutiérrez-González, C., & Puccini-Montoya, A. (2021). El entorno y la producción audiovisual en Colombia a partir del surgimiento de las OTT. *Series – International Journal of TV Serial Narratives, 7*(2), 73–86. https://doi.org/10.6092/issn.2421-454X/13318

Uribe-Jongbloed, E., & Pis Diez, E. (2017). The TV format market in Latin America: Trends and opportunities. *International Journal of Digital Television, 8*(1), 99–115. https://doi.org/10.1386/jdtv.8.1.99

# 3 The product tenet

## Content of universal appeal

Some media products have travelled well between markets while most of them never leave their original market. Products tend to travel better within similar markets (see Chapter 2), understood as those that share a history, language, tradition, colonial past, or other forms of cultural similitude. But on occasion there are products which travel beyond the expected markets and reach other spaces where they are enjoyed as well, despite cultural differences.

Products are often modified and repurposed for their new markets. This is a process often defined as localisation. This could include relatively simple modifications that are added onto the product, as in the case of subtitles for audiovisual products, or major alterations leading to adaptations, appropriations, remakes, or the development of a local version of an international television format. The process takes many shapes (addressed in detail in Chapter 5): Video games might include some of the menus translated into a variety of languages, although they maintain their in-game elements in the original language; films are dubbed and edited for a given market following national demands about content; books are translated and translator notes might be included to explain certain aspects regarding the choices made; whereas in some markets it is customary for TV shows to keep the original soundtrack with a single superimposed audio track with audio description. More radical transformations include creating a version in the new market similar to the original one, as in the adaptation of international formats (see Chalaby, 2012, 2015, 2016), or a considerable alteration that only keeps some key elements of the original work. The decision-making process of what products to bring into a different market and how to modify them is usually down to cultural transductors (explained in Chapter 4) or gatekeepers, as they have been oftentimes known. Based on the product they aim to bring into a different market, they make choices of what to keep and what no remove or modify and in which way. The central aspect is that the products themselves contain a series of qualities that are worth maintaining and others need to be adjusted. Those specific qualities are the ones that are addressed in the following pages.

DOI: 10.4324/9781003380221-3

## Traits that prompt or hinder travelling between markets

There are characteristics of a product that might enable for it to travel between markets easily, or which may constrain the markets where it can be deployed. Products that travel well have been deemed *shareable* (Singal & Udornpin, 1997), in the sense that they can be understood by different cultures and, thus, become shared between them. Products might be easy to share between culturally proximate markets because elements in the content could be easily decodified or comprehended across borders (as pointed at in Chapter 2), including the form in which they were developed. However, there are other elements that may help determine whether a product would travel well to a different market or not, including the way the product is made, how the product enters the new market and how it lends itself to be adjusted for comprehension by its new location.

Those aspects that render a product incomprehensible or irrelevant for another market are defined by Rohn (2011) as exhibiting *cultural lacunae*, whereas those products that are easily accepted and enjoyed in other cultural markets include *cultural universals* (see Table 3.1). In other words, lacunae account for the reasons why a given product might not be incorporated into a cultural market, whereas universals would be the characteristics that render it suitable for travelling to a different market.

### *Cultural lacunae: hindrances to market entry*

There are many reasons why a product would not find it easy to enter a different cultural market. It could be the language used, the topics addressed, the production values evident in the development of the product, the references incorporated, or a combination of all these factors. Cultural discount (see Chapter 2), the loss of value for the product when entering a different cultural market, is predicated upon those factors that produce cultural lacunae between origin and destination markets.

Rohn (2011) mentions three types of lacunae: content, capital, and production lacunae. Content lacunae refer to what the product is about, how it is structured and how it is supposed to be enjoyed. Capital lacunae refer to the specific knowledge, information or recognition of elements that needs to exist to enjoy the product. Production lacunae refer to the barriers that arise to accept a product based on the production values and aesthetic or stylistic qualities of the given product.

*Table 3.1* Types of cultural lacunae and cultural universals (Based on Rohn, 2011)

| Types of Cultural Lacunae | Types of Cultural Universals |
| --- | --- |
| Content lacunae | Content universals |
| Capital lacunae | Audience-created universals |
| Production lacunae | Company-created universals |

For instance, it could be imagined that in a culture where lying would be completely abhorred any TV game show that would require bluffing would be considered inappropriate[1], because "frequently, though, regional or local culture will deem specific subjects and situations taboo and will not entertain them on local television screens" (Moran, 2009, p. 125). Certain types of radio shows based on pranks might not be incorporated in cultures where the act of pranking would be considered childish or unacceptable. People might reject TV shows based on disturbing or gross content and fail to accept them as worth broadcasting. Social values and cultural mores have an impact here, as certain markets may reject or abhor some types of content. For instance, it has been seen that "content factors on box office revenues demonstrate that violence does sell, but sex (and other morally loaded content elements) does not in the context of international film markets" (Feng & Luo, 2022, p. 16), showing the type of content lacunae that might engender cultural discount on a given product. These lacunae might lead to censorship in the form of excessive editing of the products in certain markets (see Elouardaoui, 2011, for an example in Morocco; and Pakar & Khoshsaligheh, 2021, for one in Iran). Those are all forms of content lacunae.

The case for capital lacunae rests on different premises related to the cultural capital of the market consuming the product. Even if people in different countries share a language, different varieties of the language render some content as unintelligible, and this has a big impact on the shareability of products based on humour. Although the structure and function of a crossword puzzle game like *Scrabble* could be easily played in different settings, the number of letters and their value are based on the English language and do not work for other European languages, even if they use the same alphabet. Video games and game shows highly dependent on local knowledge would render themselves impossible to understand in other cultures, as is the case for dramas structured around locations, items and names that are commonplace within one culture. Moreover, Netflix has produced more drama than comedy, "may be due to a strategic response to its international postulation, which derives from the cultural limitations and complications implicit in the humour intrinsic to comedies" (Hidalgo-Marí et al., 2021, p. 11), providing evidence of how capital lacuna relates to cultural discount.

Finally, production lacunae arise when people in a different cultural market are not used to the way a certain product is presented. It could be the reading pattern of a comic book, the lighting and feel for a TV show, or the rhythm, length and pitches of a song. The form of a media product renders it unacceptable in a given cultural context because

> unlike Capital Lacunae, which include the phenomenon where audiences do not understand particular foreign media content because they lack the culturally dependent knowledge of its genre, Production Lacunae include the phenomenon where audiences do understand the genre, but simply do not enjoy it, or dislike the loosening of familiar genre rules.
>
> (Rohn, 2011, p. 635)

The three types of lacunae can be easily spotted in products and prevent these products from being deployed in other cultural markets. In fact, many companies already know of these potential lacunae and provide strategies to prevent the lacunae from taking place by suggesting the avoidance of local or specific settings or items included in scripts, in the case of TV formats (Uribe-Jongbloed & Pis Diez, 2017), or addressed and supplemented via external processes embedded in the adaptation or localisation efforts, such as a replacing a reference to Gilligan, from *Gilligan's Island,* for Robinson Crusoe in a dubbing of *Forrest Gump* in Spain (Hurtado de Mendoza Azaola, 2009, pp. 77–78).

The three types of lacunae may also appear simultaneously in certain products, although the barriers move first from a content to a capital and finally to a production lacuna, as three steps that need to be addressed to overcome cultural discount. Lacunae can be assessed at different stages of the production, distribution, and consumption of cultural products and they can be addressed according to the specific lacunae found. They are part of the elements that those who participate in the process of cultural transduction (see Chapter 4) have to assess to determine the cultural discount and its impact upon the costs of adapting or modifying the context into a target market.

If lacunae are those aspects and traits that media products possess which render them incomprehensible in other cultural settings increasing their cultural discount, the opposite could be said about *universals.*

### Cultural universals: open access to other markets

Rohn (2011) defines universals as "attributes of media content, as well as of the relationship between content and audiences, that help to overcome cultural differences between the production and the consumption cultures" (p. 625). Although a universal does not imply that it is general to all markets or cultures, it highlights aspects in a product that go beyond the original market and extend to other markets which comprehend those characteristics. Rohn divides universals into three types: content universals; audience-created universals; and company-created universals.

Content universals refer to the elements that constitute a product that allow for it to be easily understood and acceptable across cultures. Aspects of central human emotions and detachment from specific cultural elements usually serve to underpin this universal. Fantasy and sci-fi productions tend to be easily understood across cultures (Olson, 1999; Mirrlees, 2013; Lee, 2006) as they are removed from cultural specificities, including in most cases specific ethnic or religious references. Some historically shared events between countries or religious observations common to certain regions allow for content to be easily distributed within them, suffering little cultural discount. Linguistic similarity and a history of Catholicism in Italy, France, Brazil, and Colombia underscore

## Box 3.1 The expanded world of *Don Camillo*

*Don Camillo* refers to the eponymous character, a smalltown Catholic priest, who is the protagonist of a series of short vignettes written by Giovanni Guareschi in post-war Italy. The series of stories were originally published in the weekly magazine *Candido*. The vignettes were eventually compiled into books, whose numerous editions included a different array of the published stories, and which were not only translated into various languages, but also adapted audiovisually. In the 1950s there were famous film adaptations of Italo-French co-production, and even a TV version broadcast in Brazil. Later, in the 1970s there would be two other Brazilian TV adaptations and in 1980 a British adaptation that was broadcast by the BBC and licensed for broadcasting in Germany. In 1983 a new film adaptation saw the light. All the adaptations until that point had maintained the story of the rural priest dealing with the stubborn and similarly hot-headed socialist mayor, *Peppone*, in a small town on the banks of the river Po, in Italy. Despite being filmed in Portuguese, French or English, the story in the TV shows and films kept the location unaltered. A different thing happened with the 1987 Colombian adaptation of *Don Camillo*, which moved the story to the Colombian countryside of the 1950s. Because of the availability and exposure to some if not all of the different versions, Daniel Samper Pizano (see Box Text 4.1) did not only adapt the books he had read, but also indirectly the films he had watched as a kid. This process of bringing together various versions to inform the adaptation, recognising the existence of previous forms or borrowings spread historically when looking at modern adaptations of classics, is an example of the elements that make up the transmedia cultural history model proposed by Swydky (2023).

The qualities of the original vignettes written by Giovanni Guareschi that enabled its transferral into book form, translation into a variety of languages, and adaptation into film and television, highlights its cultural universality, at least for a general Western, Christian and mostly Romance-speaking public. As a curiosity, the least appreciated version by the rights holders was the British adaptation, whose rights were retracted, and thus is only available for private screening at the BFI archive in London.

For further reference on *Don Camillo* and its iterations, check:

Bandini, E., Casamatti, G. & Conti, G. (Eds). (2008). *Guareschi. Le Burrascose Avventure Di Giovannino Guareschi Nel Mondo Del Cinema*. Monte Università Parma.

Boller, R. (2014). *Don Camillo Und Peppone. Die Filme mit Fernandel und Gino Cervi von 1952 bis 1970*. Schwarzkopf & Schwarzkopf Verlag.

Espinosa-Medina, H. D., & Uribe-Jongbloed, E. (2016). "Do it, but do it dancing!": Television and format adaptations in Colombia in the 1980s and early 1990s. In K. Aveyard & A. Moran (Eds.), *New patterns in global television formats*. (pp. 125–139). Intellect.

Uribe-Jongbloed, E., & Corredor Aristizábal, M. A. (2019). The adaptation of Don Camillo through the cultural transduction framework: From Italian bestseller to a Franco-Italian film to a Colombian TV series. *Adaptation, 12*(1), 44–57. https://doi.org/10.1093/adaptation/apy020

why the characters and stories of *Don Camillo* (see Box 3.1) travelled favourably between those countries. These same reasons, linguistic and religious commonalities, explain how some products have easy travels through world regions, be that telenovelas through Latin America (Straubhaar, 1991; Medina & Barrón, 2010) or a regional version of an international format, such as the use of English for *Big Brother Africa* (Nkosi Ndela, 2013). Curiously enough, stereotyping of other cultures might serve as a content universal. In the consumption of European crime series, audiences were critical of the portrayal of stereotypical roles within their domestic production, yet seemed to be drawn by that stereotype when placed upon their European neighbours (Bengesser et al., 2023), perhaps because "the exposure to mediated stereotypes about our neighbours creates a sense of familiarity that lowers the threshold for engaging with European content" (p. 162). It is clearly problematic to use stereotypes as a content universal, but undoubtedly it has also come about because of the stereotyped media representations of cultures and nations.

Audience-created universals are dependent on the interaction of audiences or consumers with the products, in a way that they can reconstruct, modify or adapt their own interpretation to the elements provided by the product. Perhaps the most international case is when songs are performed by people who do not speak the language of the original but adapt the song to their own language possibilities[2]. When products are transparent enough and allow for multiple decoding of the motivation of the characters, audience might take a step to fill in the voids and create their own cultural explanations for actions that would otherwise be misunderstood. Incorporating audience interests and participation has been key to the development of many video games, which enable audiences and consumers to become part of the products and overcome cultural discounts by relying on their own experiences. Sometimes fan anticipation discussions around the process also help insert the products within their new markets, as has been the case for the US *Skam Austin* remake of the Norwegian series *Skam* (Bachmann, 2021).

Company-created universals refer to the construction of ancillary or paratextual materials that surround the cultural products in a way that bridges the potential lacunae of the product when entering a different cultural market. It is a strategic action that may be carried out by companies wishing to incorporate culturally external products and

> publishers such as publishing houses or television stations, and transmitters such as book retailers or cable operators, may strategically position foreign media so as to divert the audience's attention away from possible Lacunae and/or to call their attention to possible Content Universals.
>
> (Rohn, 2011, p. 637)

In fact, when specific companies have already created and defined a style which has received certain attention, any product may be created based on that company-created universal and use it to ensure that it is recognisable from that perspective. Doing a *Discovery*- or *BBC*-style documentary would be an example of this universal, which could be defined further as discourse (or discursive) proximity (Uribe-Jongbloed & Espinosa-Medina, 2014; Larkey, 2018, 2021). This discursive proximity might be achieved via different strategies including bundling (in the case of TV shows) or block booking (for films). Larkey (2018) has argued that "though aesthetic styles may be transnationally standardized and seemingly universal, sometimes barely perceptible changes in modal configurations may be deployed to produce ideologically diverging televisual narratives in each iteration of the format" (p. 20), generating specific discourse proximity to the local broadcaster. Along the same line, in a recent study on the consumption of European crime series, direct comparison to Anglo-American content is undeniable as parameters of suspenseful storytelling and compelling characters (Bengesser et al., 2023). These are clear discourses that demand proximity for success.

Similarly, Jung and Li (2014) contend that the success of the music video of *Gangnam Style* by PSY was predicated upon

> a combination of several factors: (a) the active role of K-pop fans, (b) the subsequent participation of global audiences that created a bandwagon effect, (c) PSY's marketing strategy to enforce a noninfringement copyright policy, (d) the textual hooks of the video, and (e) PSY and his company's regular promotional efforts. It is the dynamics of all these factors that produced the success of [Gangnam Style].
>
> (p. 2805)

In the case of *Gangnam Style* factors (a) and (b) are clearly seen under audience-created universals, whereas (c) and (e) are company-created universals, and (d) presents an example of content universal.

### Addressing universals and lacunae from the start

Many products are designed from the onset to be distributed in more than one cultural market. As pointed out by Bernal-Merino (2016) for the case of video games, localisation of media products is something that is no longer seen as a process undertaken after production is finished, but rather as part of the production, to ensure that adjustments made to overcome cultural lacunae are directly incorporated into the finished product. The same has been the case for Hollywood films in China (Song, 2018), and also for other markets, including the Latin America version of *Inside Out* including all in-text captions or signs in Spanish (Uribe-Jongbloed et al., 2016, p. 146).

Creators of content might already have in mind a variety of cultural markets where they want their products or services to be consumed. When this is the case, they might explore possibilities of incorporating a great number of universals and discard potential lacunae during their creative process. That is the case of the video game series *Kingdom Rush* by the Uruguayan *Ironhide Game Studio* (see Box 3.2). The first game of the series was published in 2011 for portable screens (i.e. tablets and mobile phones), and it was all in English, with a fantasy-medieval setting, cartoonish characters and ample references to contemporary Anglo-American pop culture embedded in the

---

**Box 3.2 *Kingdom Rush* by Ironhide Game Studio**

Ironhide Game Studio is located in the Uruguay capital, Montevideo. Their first great international success was *Kingdom Rush* (KR), a video game originally devised for portable screens (i.e. tablets and mobile phones) which came out in 2011. Classified under the genre of tower defence games, the objective is simple: prevent swaths of creatures from reaching a point in the screen, by spending your resources building four types of towers in predefined spaces. Its distinguishing qualities were its cartoonish characters – something also present in the company's logo which seems to resemble a turtle (see Figure 3.1), its fantasy setting, easy playability, and various references to Anglo-American popular culture. The game was a great success with over ten million downloads from Google Play alone and an assessment of 4.7 stars, earning a variety of accolades (e.g. Game of the Year 2011 by Jayisgames).

KR was clearly looking for cultural universals both in its fantasy setting and using the Anglo-American conventions, language (English) and pop culture references. There was nothing in the gameplay or within the game that would be a tell-tale of the products origin, apart from the credits. The game, for all intents and purposes, could have been made in any English-speaking country, although it was anchored on mostly American accents and references.

*Figure 3.1* Ironhide game studio logo. Courtesy of Ironhide Game Studio.

The decision was conscious on the part of the company to try to tap into a larger market than would be achieved by making it culturally linked to its place of origin. In considering the target market as international and the universality of the English language and the fantasy setting from the onset, Ironhide was not aiming to reach the Spanish-speaking market of Latin America as their primary target audience.

Despite being originally available exclusively in English, by 2023 KR already included versions with menus and written texts translated into other languages and had moved to include other videogaming platforms, such as Xbox and Steam, among others. The game is now available in ten languages (although gameplay audio files remain exclusively in English), including two versions of Chinese (simplified and traditional), six European languages (Spanish, German, French, English, Russian and Portuguese), Korean and Japanese. It consists now of four different instalments in the series *Kingdom Rush, KR Frontiers* (2013)*, KR Origins* (2014) and *KR Vengeance* (2018), with some of them earning similar or superior praise to the first one.

Their addition of a variety of Easter eggs within the gameplay has also been considered one of their many attractive traits. Through them they managed to incorporate elements beyond their original Anglo-American pop culture, such as a reference to *Obelix* a character from the French comics *Asterix* (Gozini & Uderzo) and the sculpture of The Fingers (also known as The Hand), a monument in the city of Punta del Este in their country of Uruguay. These Easter eggs provide a set of connections that allow for better rapport with different types of audiences, linking them to the product.

*Kingdom Rush* is a clear example of a product conceived to become as universal as possible in content, audience-created and company-created universals. Yet, despite that interest, localisation in terms of menus and in-game texts signal that there were still some lacunae that needed to be overcome to reach some markets.

Further discussions about Ironhide and the *Kingdom Rush* series can be found in:

Espinosa-Medina, H. D., & Uribe-Jongbloed, E. (2017). Latin American contraflow in global entertainment media: Kingdom Rush series and Zambo Dende as de-localised media products. *Media International Australia, 163*(1), 107–121. https://doi.org/10.1177/1329878X16686204

Uribe-Jongbloed, E., Espinosa-Medina, H. D., & Biddle, J. (2016). Cultural transduction and intertextuality in video games: An analysis of three international case studies. In C. Duret & C.-M. Pons (Eds.), *Contemporary research on intertextuality in video games* (pp. 143–161). IGI Glopal. https://doi.org/10.4018/978-1-5225-0477-1.ch009

game (Uribe-Jongbloed et al., 2016; Espinosa-Medina & Uribe-Jongbloed, 2017). Through the removal or reduction of culturally bound markers, such as accents, dialects, and references to local delicacies, customs, or places (see Uribe-Jongbloed & Pis-Diez, 2017, pp. 107–108; Piñón, 2014, pp. 661–665), companies looking to have their products travel internationally aim for reducing the possible lacunae at the earliest stages of development and, if required, include localisation practices early on in their development.

Whether this process stems from multinational financing that aims at having multiple countries making the product available to their audiences, as in the case of TV coproductions (see Davis & Nadler, 2010), or films looking to take advantage of national incentives and tax rebates, or an interest in regional markets beyond the national sphere – as might be the case with international content streamers or video game platforms doing simultaneous release or their products, there is a conscious process of trying to ensure that the products enjoy as much universal appeal as possible, while limiting potential cultural discount. Notwithstanding, products are seldom designed in such a way, with many of them requiring processes of adaptation or modification to suit local or regional cultural interests or requirements defined by legislation, trade, or cultural barriers (see Chapter 2). In those cases, products need to undertake one form of another of cultural transduction to accommodate the interests of the expected audience, at least from the perspective of those who want to introduce the product to the cultural market (see Chapter 4). If the products contain cultural lacunae but clearly show potential in other markets, there are different processes of adaptation to be undertaken to make them appealing in other cultural settings (see Chapter 5).

## The cultural characteristics of media products

This chapter has presented ways to define the characteristics of cultural and media products that render them easier to travel or that signal a need for an intended modification if they are to be deployed elsewhere. Clearly, it is unlikely that a product would be able to insert into a different cultural market without at least some form of intervention, even if it is not a major one. Take, for instance, a movie exhibited in cinemas in English in both the US and the UK. Usually, linguistic similarities between the versions of English might not require any modification of the film, enough cultural proximity and historical exchange between the countries implies little to no difference in film classification boards, and relatively low difference in taste. However, even in such a case, a film like *Dungeons and Dragons: Honor among Thieves* (Goldstein & Daley, 2023) has the word *Honor* changed into *Honour* for the UK release in the title and all associated images. A minimal, yet exemplary modification that shows how nuanced a review of cultural universals and lacunae are.

Analysing the lacunae and universals allows for a comprehensive evaluation of the cultural discount of a product and signal the amount of dedication and effort that would need to be applied to make the product amenable to a different audience. Sometimes the transformations that the product might undergo are aimed at overcoming some of the market or cultural barriers (see Chapter 2), rather than responding to real cultural sensibilities, as shown by the case of how films overcame the limitations of the Hays code in Hollywood by altering the epoch where the stories took place in the adaptation (Cattrysse, 2017).

In the cases where the products have not been successful in their market of origin, because they have yet to be available or because they have been directly inserted into the global market to begin with, as was the case for the international sale of *Lalola*, a format by Dori Media (Pis-Díez & García, 2014), and the case of the video game *Kingdom Rush* (see Box 3.2) there cannot be an assessment of cross-cultural predictability to determine the potential success of the product, and it all rests on the ability of those involved in the cultural transduction to determine whether it would succeed in the target market.

Now, having understood both the market distances and proximities, and the specific qualities that may enable or constrain travel, it is important to consider the people involved in the decision-making processes of cultural transduction. They are those who determine what products travel, they assess the extent of the potential cultural discount by considering the cultural lacunae, and work for ways to overcome it. They make up the people tenet (see Chapter 4) of the cultural transduction framework. It is in their actions that we can see how cultural lacunae and universals are measured, appraised, and modified to suit the interests of different markets.

## Notes

1 For instance, the successful game format *Nada más que la verdad* (2007), which managed to be sold to over 50 countries, was quickly cancelled in Colombia, where it was presented for the first time, because the way it was dealing with bringing to light lies that people had kept from their loved ones was deemed unacceptable, and a liability and mental health risk for participants (see Gómez-Restrepo, 2007).

2 When the British band *Twister Sisters* played in Chile, they accepted the rendition of their song *We're not gonna take it* as *Huevos con aceite* (Eggs with oil), which is how most Chileans sing the chorus to the song.

## References

Bachmann, A. (2021). Hankering for iconic moments: Transduction and representation in skam fans' anticipations about the remake skam austin. *Journal of Scandinavian Cinema, 11*(1), 133–147. https://doi.org/10.1386/jsca_00043_1

Bengesser, C., De Rosa, P., Jensen, P. M., & Spalletta, M. (2023). Audiences of popular European television crime drama: A nine-country study on consumption patterns, attitudes and drivers of transcultural connection. *European Journal of Communication, 38*(2), 148–165. https://doi.org/10.1177/02673231221112535

Bernal Merino, M. Á. (2016). Glocalization and co-creation. Trends in international game production. In A. Esser, M. Á. Bernal Merino, & I. R. Smith (Eds.), *Media across borders. Localizing TV, films and video games* (pp. 202–220). Routledge.

Chalaby, J. K. (2016). Drama without drama: The late rise of scripted TV formats. *Television & New Media, 17*(1), 3–20. https://doi.org/10.1177/1527476414561089

Chalaby, J. K. (2015). The advent of the transnational TV format trading system: A global commodity chain analysis. *Media, Culture & Society, 37*(3), 460–478. https://doi.org/10.1177/0163443714567017

Chalaby, J. K. (2012). At the origin of a global industry: The TV format trade as an Anglo-American invention. *Media, Culture & Society, 34*(1), 36–52. https://doi.org/10.1177/0163443711427198

Davis, C. H., & Nadler, J. (2010). International television co-productions and the cultural discount: The case of family biz, a comedy. *9th World Media Management and Economics Conference.* http://www.ryerson.ca/~c5davis/publications/Nadler-Davis-International Television Coproduction v7-12May2010.pdf

Elouardaoui, O. (2011). American series in Morocco: The adaptation process and its limitations. *Amity Journal of Media & Communication Studies, 1*(2), 18–23.

Espinosa-Medina, H. D., & Uribe-Jongbloed, E. (2017). Latin American contraflow in global entertainment media: Kingdom Rush series and Zambo Dende as delocalised media products. *Media International Australia, 163*(1), 107–121. https://doi.org/10.1177/1329878X16686204

Feng, G. C., & Luo, N. (2022). Do sex and violence sell internationally? A moderating role of cultural differences in the mediation effect of age ratings on the relationship between films' content elements and worldwide box office performance. *International Communication Gazette, 0*(0), 1–21. https://doi.org/10.1177/17480485221144593

Goldstein, J. & Daley, J. F. (Directors). (2023). *Dungeons & Dragons: Honor among Thieves* (Film). Paramount Pictures.

Gómez-Restrepo. C. (2007). "Nada más que la verdad": muchos cuestionamientos, pocas respuestas, pocas acciones. *Universitas Médica* 48(4), 437-451.

Hidalgo-Marí, T., Segarra-Saavedra, J., & Palomares-Sánchez, P. (2021). In-depth study of Netflix original content of fictional series. Forms, styles and trends in the new streaming scene. *Communication and Society, 34*(3), 1–13. https://doi.org/10.15581/003.34.3.1-13

Hurtado de Mendoza Azaola, I. (2009). Translating proper names into Spanish: The case of Forrest Gump. In J. Diaz Cintas (Ed.), *New trends in audiovisual translation* (pp. 70–82). Multilingual Matters.

Jung, S. & Le, H. (2014). Global production, circulation, and consumption of gangnam style. *International Journal of Communication, 8*, 2790–2810.

Larkey, E. (2018). Narratological approaches to multimodal cross-cultural comparisons of global TV formats. *View Journal of European Television History and Culture, 7*(14), 1–21.

Larkey, E. (2021). German narratives in international television format adaptations: Comparing du und ich (ZDF 2002) with un gars, une fille (Quebec 1997–2002). *Digital Humanities Quarterly, 15*(1), 1–18.

Lee, F. L. F. (2006). Cultural discount and cross-culture predictability: Examining the box office performance of American movies in Hong Kong. *Journal of Media Economics, 19*(4), 259–278. https://doi.org/10.1207/s15327736me1904_3

Medina, M., & Barrón, L. (2010). La telenovela en el mundo. *Palabra Clave, 13*(1), 77–97.

Mirrlees, T. (2013). *Global entertainment media. Between cultural imperialism and cultural globalization.* Routledge.

Moran, A. (2009). *New flows in global TV.* Intellect.

Nkosi Ndlela, M. (2013). Television across boundaries: Localisation of big brother Africa. *Critical Studies in Television: An International Journal of Television Studies, 8*(2), 57–72. https://doi.org/10.7227/CST.8.2.6

Olson, S. R. (1999). *Hollywood planet: Global media and the compettitive advantage of narrative transparency.* Lawrence Erlbaum Associates, Inc.

Pakar, E. & Khoshsaligheh, M. (2021). Cultural mediation and gatekeeping in dubbing of American feature films on Iranian television. *Journal of Intercultural Communication Research, 50*(5), 459–480. https://doi.org/10.1080/17475759.2021.1954541

Piñón, J. (2014). Reglocalization and the rise of the network cities media system in producing telenovelas for hemispheric audiences. *International Journal of Cultural Studies, 17*(6), 655–671. https://doi.org/10.1177/1367877913515867

Pis Diez, E., & García, F. (2014). El desarrollo del mercado audiovisual en Argentina: una industria de exportación. *Palabra Clave, 17*(4), 1137–1167. https://doi.org/10.5294/pacla.2014.17.4.7

Rohn, U. (2011). Lacuna or universal? Introducing a new model for understanding crosscultural audience demand. *Media Culture Society, 33*(4), 631–641. https://doi.org/10.1177/0163443711399223

Singhal, A., & Udornpim, K. (1997). Cultural shareability, archetypes and television soaps. *Gazette, 59*(3), 171–188.

Song, X. (2018). Journey to the east: A review of Hollywood's film localization efforts for China's film market. *International Journal of English and Cultural Studies, 2*(1), 1. https://doi.org/10.11114/ijecs.v2i1.3872

Szwydky, L. L. (2023). CODA: Transmedia cultural history, convergence culture and the future of adapatation studies. In L.L. Szwydky & G. Jellenik (Eds.), *Adaptation before cinema: Literary and visual convergence from antiquity through the nineteenth century* (pp. 283–303). PalgraveMacmillan. https://doi.org/10.1007/978-3-031-09596-2_13

Uribe-Jongbloed, E., Espinosa-Medina, H. D., & Biddle, J. (2016). Cultural transduction and intertextuality in video games: An analysis of three international case studies. In C. Duret & C.-M. Pons (Eds.), *Contemporary research on intertextuality in video games* (pp. 143–161). IGI Glopal. https://doi.org/10.4018/978-1-5225-0477-1.ch009

Uribe-Jongbloed, E., & Pis Diez, E. (2017). The TV format market in Latin America: Trends and opportunities. *International Journal of Digital Television, 8*(1), 99–115. https://doi.org/10.1386/jdtv.8.1.99

# 4 The people tenet

## The jobs making cultural and media products travel between markets

Many of the cultural and media products we consume on a daily basis hail from a different cultural market. Whether it is the songs, podcasts, or radio programmes we listen to, the movies, series, and videos we watch, the comics or books we read and the video games we play. In most cases, we consume them in a form that is closer to our local culture, translated, dubbed, or subtitled, even remade in our own vicinity. But seldom do we stop to think how the product came to reach us. We now understand that products easily travel to markets that are close in cultural traits, because of cultural proximity (see Chapter 2), and because of some of the qualities of the products render them attractive, interesting, and enjoyable for our culture – or at least by the part of the culture that enjoys the cultural capital to understand them (see Chapter 3). But products do not just appear on our doorsteps, TV screens or mobile phones out of the blue. There are people who have intervened to ensure that a certain product or media offering reaches an intended audience. The way it has been done has included, for most part of our history, the import of material over physical borders. Movies and TV shows were transported in cans of film or videotapes, music in cylinders or plastic disks and tapes, books, and magazines on bound paper, and works of art in whichever material form contained them. But people also carried with them impressions, notes, and memories of experiences they had which would help develop other products. Whether it was by taking inspiration or blatant poaching of other products, people engaged with bridging the gap, taking stories, songs, game show ideas, and letting them take hold in a different setting.

It is these people, and their roles in the process of cultural transduction (see Chapter 1, for the definition), which is the focus of this chapter. The categories under which we study them here are not correspondent to the job titles and tasks currently deployed in the audiovisual industry (see García Avis & Diego, 2018), but they serve to understand the conceptual processes developed by these people in deciding what products are worth bringing over borders. Those decision-makers have been addressed by many names, including gatekeepers, cultural intermediaries (Waisbord & Jalfin, 2009; Khaire, 2017) or arbiters (Bielby, 2011) and, perhaps more recently, influencers. From the

DOI: 10.4324/9781003380221-4

travelling gallery collector to the head of formats acquisition or the translator in charge of localising a video game, these people engage with the selection, distribution, and alteration of cultural products to profit from cultural proximity and universality, and reduce cultural lacunae, to improve understanding, enjoyment, and, in many cases, consumption in a target market. Cultural transductors are a type of cultural intermediary that is concerned with products that cross or that could cross, according to their appreciation, cultural borders. Those "intermediaries connect artworks and consumers through their discourse; without intermediaries' discourse, consumers would find it difficult, if not impossible, to discover, understand, and evaluate cultural goods such as artworks" (Khaire, 2017, p. 53), but for the case of cultural transductors, they are concerned with those products that stem from a different cultural space. For instance,

> when a marketer says a game will not sell in the United States, or when a translator changes a joke to make it more "culturally appropriate," they become a kind of gatekeeper, shaping and channeling (and sometimes preventing entirely) the transnational circulation of these stories and images. Thus, it seems especially important to examine the contexts and consequences of these decision-making practices.
>
> (Carlson & Corliss, 2011, pp. 64–65)

The decisions of these cultural transductors have impacts upon the insertion or lack thereof of cultural products into other markets.

Not always are they engaged with paid work in their endeavours. Some might do it out of personal interest to share an enjoyable experience they had with another product, as were the hundreds of mix cassette tapes made for friends or fan-dubbings of *anime* shows, while others work in one of the cultural or creative industries that require the output and consumption of great quantities of production, leading to copycats (see Thomas, 2006), format negotiations, adaptations, and dubbings, among many other transformations.

For the discussion, an earlier work on cultural transduction classified these people into three distinct roles: the scout, the merchant, and the alchemist (Uribe-Jongbloed & Espinosa-Medina, 2014, p. 39). Those roles refer, basically, to the actions of looking for, negotiating and modifying cultural products between different cultural markets.

## The scout

A scout is any person who has selected cultural products from one market to insert them into another one. Usually, the scouts consider that they possess sufficient inside knowledge of the target culture to select a product that would easily insert itself into the cultural market. They select the product because of the potential they see, often thinking about how easy it would be for the product to overcome any cultural barriers. Occasionally, the process stems from a personal interest (see Box 4.1), but it could also be a general appreciation of potential cross-cultural predictability (see Chapters 2 and 3). DJs bringing music into their radio shows, or club performances, are a good example of scouts, who select material and present it to an audience based on how they believe their personal taste relates to that of their audiences.

---

**Box 4.1 A Jack-of-all-trades: Daniel Samper Pizano as cultural transductor**

Daniel Samper Pizano (b. 1945) is a journalist and writer, known for his work in Colombian media. Apart from his accolades in journalism, he was fundamental in a variety of cultural products in Colombia. His weekly humorous columns in magazines part of the newspaper *El Tiempo* in the 1970s were compiled in the book *Dejémonos de vainas* (1978), which was adapted into a treatment for a television weekly comedy-soap opera show of the same name, with the first four years of its 14-year broadcast (1984–1998) scripted and directed by Bernardo Romero Pereiro (Uribe-Jongbloed & Roncallo-Dow, 2021).

After creating one of the most famous TV shows in the country and in the same partnership with Romero Pereiro, in the late 1980s, Samper Pizano was also responsible for proposing (as a scout), acquiring the rights (alongside Romero Pereiro acting both as merchants), and then developing the treatment (with Romero Pereiro writing the scripts) of the Colombian TV adaptation of *Don Camillo* (see Box 3.2; Uribe-Jongbloed & Corredor Aristizabal, 2019).

Apart from that, he had also been instrumental in selecting (again as a scout), and arranging the publication for a Colombian newspaper (as a merchant) in the 1980s and early 1990s of the comic strip *Boogie, el aceitoso* by the Argentinian writer, humourist, and cartoonist, Roberto Fontanarrosa (Uribe-Jongbloed et al., 2019).

His achievements in investigative journalism and his impact in creating one of the most famous and longest-lasting television shows in the country would be enough for Samper Pizano to be remembered. But his effort to bring other cultural capital into Colombia exemplifies the impact of cultural transductors as gatekeepers that recognise, negotiate and introduce products from one cultural market into another.

Further discussion of Daniel Samper Pizano's role as cultural transductor:

Uribe-Jongbloed, E., & Corredor Aristizábal, M. A. (2019). The adaptation of Don Camillo through the cultural transduction framework: From Italian Bestseller to Franco-Italian Film to a Colombian TV series. *Adaptation, 12*(1), 44–57. https://doi.org/10.1093/adaptation/apy020

Uribe-Jongbloed, E., Aguilar Rodríguez, D., & Suárez, F. (2019). Boogie, el aceitoso en la Colombia de los 80 y 90: el negro Fontanarrosa, Samper Pizano y el miedo al falso héroe. *Journal of Iberian and Latin American Research, 25*(3), 244–257. https://doi.org/10.1080/13260219.2019.1740455

Uribe-Jongbloed, E. & Roncallo-Dow, S. (2021). Dejémonos de vainas, ¡sí? YouTube como memoria y archivo televisivo colombiano. In J. C. Henao & M. A. Pinzón Camargo (Eds.), *¿Cuarta revolución industrial? Contribuciones tecnosociales para la transformación social. Disrupción tecnológica, transformación y sociedad* (pp. 499–524). Universidad Externado de Colombia.

Similar to sports scouts who travel across countries looking for the young new players to recruit for their teams, the cultural transductor working as a scout might be engaged in the negotiation of the product – in the case of optionees buying adaptation rights–, or may skip it altogether. That was the case for most appropriations and copies of radio and TV shows from the US by those entrepreneurs from other places travelling there and catching a morning show on the radio or *The Price is Right* on television broadcasts, and creating local versions without any acknowledgement of the original (see Uribe-Jongbloed & Espinosa-Medina, 2016). In the global trade of television shows, "buyers keep up with new developments in the international field, scout new shows, watch new programmes and formats and generally look out for interesting content around the world" (Kuipers, 2012, p. 587).

The scout is a similar category to that of pioneer-intermediaries (see Khaire, 2017, pp. 95–96), although the latter might include scouts working within one culture, rather than between them, who discover something they consider others in the same market would appreciate, if appropriately nudged. In some areas more than others, people could dedicate actively to scouting, even if only through reading trade magazines for important hits in other parts of the world that might result in a worthy negotiation of rights. By looking for hits elsewhere, they assess the cross-cultural predictability to define if it is worth acquiring those products for a different market.

Although scouts tend to disappear in established trades by becoming part of the merchants, they might still exist in the form of influencers that bring attention to products from other locales through their internet platforms. As the trading processes of media content become more amply formalised between markets, being a scout becomes part of structured teams in charge of acquisitions and sales, but they remain fundamental in ensuring that other products which have not reached the level of formal trade travel between borders.

# The merchant

Whereas a scout discovers cultural or media products which could be success-ful in a different market, merchants engage with the negotiations and trade processes to ensure that the result becomes a profitable enterprise. In the de-veloped markets of comics, film, and television there are various international fairs and conventions where executives from production companies world-wide engage in negotiations to provide all types of finished products, scripts, formats, films and where business meetings are carried out for the negotiation of adaptation or distribution rights. These places have been documented and studied amply (see Havens, 2006; Woo, 2012; Khonen, 2021; Bielby & Har-rington, 2008; Guerrero, 2010; Moran, 2009, pp. 23–42), as sites of business trades and spaces of interaction with fan audiences. Bielby (2011) found out that in those trade shows there were two types of assessment made to decide on the acquisition of a product or licensing rights, noticing that

> content of product appraisals consists of two key categories: rational, con-crete criteria that empirically signal quality and aesthetic criteria that in-voke cultural indicators of entertainment. The latter include overt claims about quality per se, expressive terminology about products, and experi-ence in the industry as a benchmark for appraisal.
>
> (p. 536)

In other words, there is an idea of an assessment of cross-cultural pre-dictability based on the success of the product in other markets and on po-tential cultural lacunae – particularly content and production lacunae – (see Chapter 3). Further, Bielby (2011) states that "buying and selling clearly entails more than just reading program descriptions; it entails analysis and interpretation of cultural adequacy in the fullest sense" (p. 537), presenting the importance of the judgement calls made by those in the trade. Similarly, Engelstad (2018) presents that from the perspective of a film producer, a type of merchant, the processes of determining what products to insert in a market as adaptation might go through the following steps:

> (1) Study the art section or trade magazines for interviews, book reviews, and sales charts; attend public readings at libraries and book festivals; and arrange meetings with editors and literary agents. (2) Find a title that can appeal to a target audience at the movies (broad or niche) and acquire the rights. (3) Estimate production costs and requirements. (4) Hire a screen-writer and a director with the desired artistic qualities to develop the pro-duction. (5) Start marketing the film, emphasizing its most potent selling points – which may not always be the source book or its author. (6) For the next film, start all over again and repeat each step.
>
> (p. 30)

Points (1) and (2) address the producer's interest in assessing cultural discount between the intended audience and the product, to evaluate the worth of the rights acquisition. Point (3) focuses on the role of the alchemist, who will be in charge of the transformation of the product. Point (5) also renders clear that sometimes being aware of the origin of the product may be desirable while sometimes it might not, and underscores the importance of developing company-created universals via marketing strategies.

Also, decisions as to what elements would work well from a business perspective may imply sacrificing other aspects that could be desirable. In the increasing transnational business of multilingual thrillers in streaming platforms, "the transformation of those series into a coveted product to be sold in the global media market eroded the commitment of the producers to represent accurate linguistic behavior" (Ribke, 2022, p. 685). Diminishing linguistic realism might have impact when presenting the product again in the original market but may increase international appeal.[1] These trade-offs are the ones assessed by the merchants to determine whether or not to engage in the insertion of a product into a given market.

Although the trading process differs from business to business in the creative and media sector, the merchant is a role played by a variety of participants, distributed among those concerned with the appreciation and assessment of products, and those in sales and acquisitions, including legal teams in charge of licencing agreements and contracts.

## The alchemist

Once a product has been acquired or licensed for a particular cultural market, or when someone has decided to insert it into it through non-conventional channels (e.g. fan-subbing in YouTube), a new role is concerned with ensuring that the existent cultural lacunae are overcome through a variety of processes. These processes might include different levels of modification of the original product, expanding from an end-of-the-pipeline intervention on the finished product (e.g. subtitles for audiovisual products), to reconstructions, adaptations, versioning, and the creation of new products that might differ considerably from the original work. The fields of translation (see Chesterman, 2009) and adaptation studies (see Hutcheon, 2013, pp. 79–111) have paid considerable attention to the roles of these people in charge of modifying a work to respond to cultural requirements of an insertion market, showing the complexity of defining them. The alchemist's role is considerably magical, because it is expected to bridge the unintelligibility of elements of a cultural product by providing a strategy that ensures it is comprehended and enjoyable within a different cultural remit. As presented by Maitland (2017), a translator's first job is to understand something that refuses to be understood (p. 9), because the role of the translator begins with approaching the original text which is deemed culturally obscure for the new intended audience. Basically, they need to turn cultural lead into gold, since

> the role of the translator – as an individual working within a specific set of audience requirements, constraints, needs and expectations to which her translation must be sensitive – requires intense ethical reflection on the relations between distant and often conflicting contingencies of text, society, people and culture.
>
> (Maitland, 2017, p. 25)

The description of a translator seems to fit exactly with that of any other cultural transductor, because it goes beyond the idea of one-to-one reproducibility of words, to an interpretation of the interconnecting elements that make up a cultural product. Whether adapting a novel into a film, creating a local version of a TV format, modifying gameplay in a video game or inserting a line of toys into a different market,[2] the transductor has to ensure that a product, regardless of its original qualities, retains enough of them to suit a given cultural taste in the insertion market.

In video game localisation, the process includes a variety of actors that span the areas of administration and management, production, and post-production (Mejías-Climent, 2021, pp. 102–109). From determining the assets to be translated, to dubbing and sound editing, or even altering audiovisual material, the alchemist must ensure that the whole retains value and interest while becoming relevant to a target market. These decisions could even take place before the intention to localise, since "many aspects of video game localization begin well before there are even any assets to translate – deciding, for example, where the game will be sold, and what languages it will be translated into" (Carlson & Corliss, 2011, p. 65). Failure to proceed with a culturally sensible expectation regarding the content might lead to a total disregard for the product.[3]

Alchemists might be part of a formal enterprise's interest in the modification process, as in the case of local scriptwriters of TV formats belonging to a production company or broadcaster, or they may be fans and enthusiasts who engage on volunteer and unpaid activity to bring a cultural product to a market where it is unavailable or unachievable (see Chapter 5). They make decisions that determine who have access to certain material from a different cultural market, because "even international channels owned by large conglomerates typically employ domestic programmers, who select programming from the international markets and schedule them based upon their own perceptions of the fit between imported programs and audience preferences" (Havens, 2007, p. 221). Similarly, with video games localisation, sometimes it is the distributors who provide the frame and requirement for the localisation process (Carlson & Corliss, 2011), and in the case of national television broadcasts, those in charge of these decisions provide their own view of "national culture" to define correct insertion (Waisbord & Jalfin, 2009), and generate the demands for "cultural appropriateness" leading to censorship (see Pakar & Khoshsaligheh, 2021).

As Esser (2016) has highlighted, it is always very difficult to define what "local" is in the process of localisation, since a variety of appreciations and cultural sensibilities are not generally and evenly distributed among any given population, and in television scholarship there is an assumption that "local is bound to territory and that the TV audience is (still) defined by national culture and state borders" (p. 20). A similar criticism of the "local" comes from Scholz and Stein (2017) who point out that other cultural spaces could be considered, such as a *game culture* that refers to those who participate collectively in international gaming platforms, and who share cultural capital, yet are not ordered by "national culture". Furthermore, "cultural differences and divides are often supported, enforced, and elaborated on by 'locals'" (Carlson & Corliss, 2011, p. 68), with a variety of interests, from cultural overzealousness to the promotion of local employment demanding that, instead of bringing foreign content, the product is remade locally,[4] because "local adaptations express gatekeepers' particular selection of themes and issues driven by profit-making concerns" (Waisbord & Jalfin, 2009, p. 69) or by local mores and religious observance (as is the case for dubbing and subtitling of American films in Iran presented by Pakar & Khoshsaligheh, 2021).

With these observations in mind, the alchemist is transforming the cultural product to one specific cultural market or group which may not necessarily be coterminous with national or other political boundaries, but following other interests.[5] Straubhaar et al. (2019) have pointed out that preferences for foreign TV productions in Latin America are linked to cosmopolitanism, higher economic affluence, elite attitudes and an omnivorous preference for the geographical origin of products, which leads them to conclude that "while Netflix, Amazon, and Disney+ may dominate the viewing of the upper-middle class, it has not yet become the mainstream of Latin American television" (p. 250). Local, then, for Latin America would imply a mediation of the sociocultural and economic conditions of the audience. Accordingly, when adapting a TV format, alchemists consider who their audience will be and if they need adjustment for a cosmopolitan taste or one that is anchored on former national production. The final decision made by alchemists tells us about their own idea of what "local" tastes and appreciation are. However, alchemists might also be constrained in their decision-making process by limitations arising from the type of content being modified, including time or space-bound possibilities in the case of dubbing and subtitling, or requirements established by the companies which own the original product being adapted.

There might be an interest in preventing localised versions from failing to achieve quality requirements set by the original product. This concern is often voiced in scripted format negotiations, which seek for the versions to keep sufficient consistency to prevent a drop of value for the brand. It is common practice for certain format owners to request a revision of the adapted scripts to ensure that they do not deviate from the instructions set up by the brand. The alchemist has to ensure that there is no loss of value for the original, while trying to bring increased value to the modified version locally, and overcome cultural discount.

## A juggler or a jack-of-all-trades?

The classification presented between the three roles does not imply that they are mutually exclusive. On many occasions, people engaging in cultural trans-duction slide between those roles or more than one person at once embrace them. Although the terms "juggler" or "jack-of-all-trades" may both seem to work to describe those who engage in all of those roles simultaneously, it becomes possible to define them as overlapping or sequential roles. In current day audiovisual product trades, or as presented above by Engelstad (2018) for film producers, selection, and negotiation might be part and parcel of the same task. Scouts might continue to find cultural products that, for lack of support or structural barriers, may not reach the interest of those who are in international trade fairs or other business spaces. Merchants may occasionally look for products themselves, or may participate in the localisation of selected products, but the role of trader already demands sufficient work that they tend to dedicate exclusively to it. Most of the job titles presented by García Avis and Diego (2018) in the production companies dealing with formats often en-gage more with acquisition or negotiation than with adaptation or localisation or vice-versa, despite there being no one-to-one relation between these roles and the job titles they have presented.

However, there are very specific cases in which all three roles could be evidenced in the case of a single individual or group of individuals (see Box 4.1). Most enterprises dedicated to localisation of video games or dubbing of audiovisual products engage with the alchemist role of the process, respond-ing to a task assigned or a request for labour, and do not usually look out for products to adapt themselves. Simultaneously, in an age of convergence and collective activity at a distance strongly supported by the internet (Jenkins, 2006; Jenkins et al., 2013), volunteers, fans, and influencers also engage in processes of cultural transduction. Formal, paid, and traditionally established businesses and media legacy outlets coexist with interests-based, unpaid, and newly developed communities participating in the selection, negotiation, dis-tribution, and modification of cultural and media products, prompting their crossing over all types of barriers (see Chapter 5). The phenomenon is not new, and similarly to transmedia (see Weedon, 2021; Scolari et al., 2014; Szwydky, 2023) or the concept of convergence (Arango-Forero et al., 2016), can be traced back as far as human media production.

The focus has been placed here on the roles which are fundamental for cultural transduction. They are similar to those that take place within a single cultural setting, in the case of those looking for, acquiring and adapting material from one medium to another, as in the literature to film adaptation industry. However, the main difference in the case of the cultural transductors, which makes them more akin to translators, is that their remit is between markets, rather than within them. The overlap necessarily exists, and if cultural markets can be also determined by the age, social class or historicity of a group, then in most cases those working within a culture might also be cultural transductors. But they never work in a vacuum. Their participation in pre-existent structures, organisations, and institutions informs and constrains their decisions as well. That provides the missing element of cultural transduction which is studied under the process tenet (see Chapter 5).

## Notes

1  That was the case of *Narcos* when consumed by Colombian audiences (Brodzinsky, 2015).
2  For a very interesting view on this issue, look at the job that was given to Jim Shooter, Denny O'Neil and Bob Budiansky to "create" the transformers for the US market (Stern & Frost, 2018).
3  Such was the case with the lack of Spanish-language dubbing with the already recognisable voices of the characters for the video game *South Park: The stick of truth* in Spain (Uribe-Jongbloed et al., 2016).
4  This could be argued for the reticence in the US of directly broadcasting UK content and instead adapting it, or the insistence in Argentina that films be dubbed locally, rather than accepting international Latin American dubbing made in the US or Mexico.
5  For instance, a relatively educated audience could be actively favourable to a lack of dubbing of languages that the main characters themselves cannot understand (Krämer & Duran Eppler, 2018).

## References

Arango-Forero, G., Roncallo-Dow, S., & Uribe-Jongbloed, E. (2016). Rethinking convergence: A new word to describe an old idea. In A. Lugmayr & C. D. Zotto (Eds.), *Media convergence handbook* (pp. 17–28). Springer. https://doi.org/10.1007/978-3-642-54484-2_2

Bielby, D. D. (2011). Staking claims: Conveying transnational cultural value in a creative industry. *American Behavioral Scientist, 55*(5), 525–540. https://doi.org/10.1177/0002764211398077

Bielby, D. D., & Harrington, C. L. (2008). *Global TV. Exporting television and culture in the world market.* New York University Press.

Brodzinsky, S. (2015). Narcos is a hit for Netflix but iffy accents grate on Colombian ears. *The Guardian.* https://www.theguardian.com/world/2015/sep/17/narcos-netflix-colombian-accents

Carlson, R., & Corliss, J. (2011). Imagined commodities: Video game localization and mythologies of cultural difference. *Games and Culture, 6*(1), 61–82. https://doi.org/10.1177/1555412010377322

Chesterman, A. (2009). The name and nature of translator studies. *Journal of Language and Communication in Business*, *22*(42), 13–22. https://doi.org/10.7146/hjlcb. v22i42.96844

Engelstad, A. (2018). Playing the producer's game: Adaptation and the question of fidelity. *Adaptation*, *11*(1), 25–39. https://doi.org/10.1093/adaptation/apx023

Esser, A. (2016). Defining 'the local' in localization, or 'adapting for whom?'. In A. Esser, M. Á. Bernal-Merino & I. R. Smith (Eds.), *Media across borders* (pp. 19–35). Routledge.

García-Avis, I., & Diego, P. (2018). Perfiles profesionales en la adaptación de series televisivas. *Palabra Clave*, *21*(2), 310–337. https://doi.org/10.5294/pacla.2018.21.2.3

Guerrero, E. (2010). El desarrollo de proyectos audiovisuales: adquisición y creación de formatos de entretenimiento. *Comunicación y Sociedad*, *23*(1), 237–273.

Havens, T. (2006). *Global television marketplace*. British Film Institute.

Havens, T. (2007). The hybrid grid: Globalization, cultural power and Hungarian television schedules. *Media, Culture & Society*, *29*(2), 219–239. https://doi.org/10.1177/0163443707074254

Hutcheon, L. (2013). *A theory of adaptation*. Routledge.

Jenkins, H. (2006). *Convergence culture: Where old and new media collide*. New York University Press.

Jenkins, H., Ford, S., & Green, J. (2013). *Spreadable media: Creating value and meaning in a network culture*. New York University Press.

Khaire, M. (2017). *Culture and commerce: The value of entrepreneurship in creative industries*. Stanford University Press.

Kohnen, M. E. S. (2021). The experience economy of TV promotion at San Diego Comic-Con. *International Journal of Cultural Studies*, *24*(1), 157–176. https://doi-org. basesbiblioteca.uexternado.edu.co/10.1177/1367877920935888

Krämer, M., & Duran Eppler, E. (2018). The deliberate non-subtitling of L3s in breaking bad: A reception study. *Meta*, *63*(2), 365–391. https://doi.org/10.7202/1055144ar

Kuipers, G. (2012). The cosmopolitan tribe of television buyers: Professional ethos, personal taste and cosmopolitan capital in transnational cultural mediation. *European Journal of Cultural Studies*, *15*(5), 581–603. https://doi.org/10.1177/1367549412445760

Maitland, S. (2017). *What is cultural translation?* Bloomsbury.

Mejías-Climent, L. (2021). *Enhancing video game localization through dubbing*. Routledge.

Moran, A. (2009). *New flows in global TV*. Intellect.

Pakar, E. & Khoshsaligheh, M. (2021): Cultural mediation and gatekeeping in dubbing of American feature films on Iranian television. *Journal of Intercultural Communication Research*, *50*(5), 459–480. https://doi.org/10.1080/17475759.2021.1954541

Ribke, N. (2022). Bilingual fiction series, genre conventions, and the economy of linguistic interaction in Israeli television. *International Journal of Cultural Studies*, *25*(6), 673–689. https://doi.org/10.1177/13678779221114380

Scholz, T. M., & Stein, V. (2017). Juxtaposing transduction and transtraction: Pugging in international virtual teams. *Palabra Clave*, *20*(3), 788–804. https://doi.org/10.5294/pacla.2017.20.3.9

Scolari, C.A., Bertetti, P. & Freeman, M. (2014). *Transmedia archaeology: Storytelling in the borderlines of science fiction, comics and pulp magazines*. Palgrave Pivot.

Stern, T. (Director) & B. J. Frost (Scriptwriter). (2018). *The toys that made us: Transformers* (S2E2) [TV show: 48 min]. The Nacelle Company and Winery Productions.

Straubhaar, J., Santillana, M., de Macedo Higgins Joyce, V, & Duarte, L. G. (2019). *From Telenovelas to Netflix: Transnational, transverse television in Latin America.* Palgrave Macmillan.

Szwydky, L. L. (2023). CODA: Transmedia cultural history, convergence culture and the future of adaptation studies. In L.L. Szwydky & G. Jellenik (Eds.), *Adaptation before cinema: Literary and visual convergence from antiquity through the nineteenth century* (pp. 283–303). PalgraveMacmillan. https://doi.org/10.1007/978-3-031-09596-2_13

Thomas, A. O. (2006). Cultural economics of TV programme cloning: Or why India has produced multi-"millionaires." *International Journal of Emerging Markets, 1*(1), 35–47. https://doi.org/10.1108/17468800610644997

Uribe-Jongbloed, E., & Espinosa-Medina, H. D. (2014). A clearer picture: Towards a new framework for the study of cultural transduction in audiovisual market trades. *Observatorio, 8*(1), 23–48. http://obs.obercom.pt/index.php/obs/article/view/707/642

Uribe-Jongbloed, E., Espinosa-Medina, H. D., & Biddle, J. (2016). Cultural transduction and intertextuality in video games: An analysis of three international case studies. In C. Duret & C.-M. Pons (Eds.), *Contemporary research on intertextuality in video games* (pp. 143–161). IGI Glopal. https://doi.org/10.4018/978-1-5225-0477-1.ch009

Waisbord, S., & Jalfin, S. (2009). Imagining the national: Gatekeepers and the adaptation of global franchises in Argentina. In A. Moran (Ed.), *TV formats worldwide. localizing global programs* (pp. 55–74).

Weedon, A. (2021). *The origins of transmedia storytelling in early twentieth century adaptation.* Palgrave Macmillan.

Woo, B. (2012). Alphanerds: Cultural intermediaries in a subcultural scene. *European Journal of Cultural Studies, 15*(5), 659–676. https://doi.org/10.1177/1367549412445758

# 5   The process tenet

## Corporate interests and fan engagement in cultural transduction

We are constantly bombarded by new media content. Much of this media content arises based on previous content that has been developed before, elsewhere or in a different medium than how we are experiencing it. In certain cases, we might be clearly aware of the source material that has inspired or been adjusted in the version we are exposed to, while many times the influences or origins have been consciously or unwittingly erased. We become at once surprised and excited, when not offended, at recognising the connection between the product we are experiencing and the one or the variety of them that are linked to it. Parody immediately comes to mind, for it is the type of content that seems to be enjoyable exclusively when the source material or elements can be clearly determined. In fact, in many countries the protection against copyright lawsuits hinges precisely on the ability to recognise the original within the parody and establishing its difference (see Uribe-Jongbloed et al., 2021; Melo Sarmiento, 2020).

In some other cases, we might experience a sense of excitement derived from understanding references that escape the rest of the audience, and we rejoice in our recognition of the intertextual elements, feeling that our specialist knowledge allows us to spot hidden meanings or convenient Easter eggs (see Uribe-Jongbloed et al., 2016; Uribe-Jongbloed & Roncallo-Dow, 2018). In other cases, it comes in as an annoyance, close to feeling cheated, by recognising the work one is exposed to might be considered derivative of other works, while not evidently presented as such. One such instance could be my personal experience with *Verliebt in Berlin* (as presented in Chapter 1), or when I watched Hansi Hinterseer's video *So sehr liebe ich dich* (2011) in YouTube.[1] The latter is a German-language version of the song *Arroyito* written by Wilfran Castillo, a Colombian songwriter, made popular by its performer Fonseca in 2008.[2] Of course, cross-pollination and translation of songs is extremely common, but my surprise came from two unexpected experiences: the first one, the fact that the song was clearly recognisable and seemed to have undergone very little alteration in its music, although considerable change in the meaning of the song due to translation; and the second, that there was no reference in the video presenting its origins, with the images depicting the singer

DOI: 10.4324/9781003380221-5

alongside a stream in what looked to be the Alps. Perhaps most interestingly, was the accordion solo, which, curiously enough, is the most evident German influence upon Colombian vallenato music. The same way that *Yo soy Betty, la fea* managed to become *Verliebt in Berlin*, Fonseca's vallenato-pop *Arroyito* became a *schlager* by Hansi Hinterseer under *So sehr liebe ich dich*. A good time before that I had felt a similar disappointment when, years after having watched *Three's company* (1977) as *Tres son compañía* in the dubbed version into Latin American Spanish in free-to-air television in Colombia, it was brought to my attention that *Three's Company* is the American version of the British show *Man about the House* (1973). Whereas the dubbing I was exposed to in the early 1980s probably robbed me of many references to Santa Monica and the interlinked gay scene, it was clear to me that the story was taking place there and I had no inkling about it being originally a story set up in London.

The cases presented above include two of the media markets we are all very aware of, the music and television industry. Undoubtedly, the processes within these industries include the acquisition of adaptation rights and the payment of copyright royalties to ensure they can modify those products for a given audience. There was a structure for the process of recognising, selecting, and acquiring products and distribution rights, probably under the activity of professionals engaged with finding and selecting (see the scouts in Chapter 4) or buying and selling (see the merchants in Chapter 4) them. There is an institutional structure concerned with bringing these products to a new market, and their formal system carries out all these processes. Whether through translation, subtitling, dubbing, voicing over, changing the editing or the format to fit different screens, acquiring scripts to be re-written, re-making, buying a format and receiving consultation, re-creating or perhaps only drawing inspiration, when not blatantly copying, different established companies dedicate to transforming these cultural products within their remit. Broadcasters, TV producers, music labels, film studios, video game workshops, publishers, and other types of media companies involve themselves in the process of cultural transduction, with staff dedicated to making those changes (see the alchemist in Chapter 4) to suit their intended audience.

At the same time, and maybe as we have all done at one point or another throughout our lives, we have done that same job when we translated the lyrics of a song to share them with friends or cover them at a soirée, added our own voice-over to videos, created stories or comics based on renowned characters, or even going as far as using Lego for stop-motion animations or even ASCII code for rendering *Star Wars: A new hope* (https://asciimation. co.nz/), with all the nostalgia it entails (Johnson, 2017). The many ways in which people have engaged with previously existing material or products and participated with it to develop their own work has been central to fan culture for many years. Despite these processes being nothing new (Arango-Forero et al., 2016; Scolari et al., 2014; Weedon, 2021; Szwydky, 2023), the internet has made it easier than ever before to share, exchange and see the results of your newly developed products. Memes have been mentioned often as the clearest evidence of the new sharing culture that takes a simple element or set of elements to create multiplicities of meaning by combining, replicating and distributing widely known or recognisable images and texts (see Uribe-Jongbloed & Mora-Moreo, 2020), sometimes obscuring the nature of the original products where these elements are drawn from (see Roncallo-Dow, 2016) and in some occasions creating willing and unwilling subjects as internationally recognisable.[3]

Both processes could be easily seen as the two faces of the same coin, one based on formal and structured media corporations that have evolved through the years with specialised markets and knowledge, and another with the volunteer and dedicated effort of fans. They are different ways in which the process of cultural translation is carried out, yet they oftentimes achieve similar results. They insert products into a market where the product was not readily available, accommodate it to their intended audience based on their cultural capital and understanding of the cultural market where they expect the product to be inserted, and make conscious decisions while doing it that may carry important results.

With the intention of describing them separately to serve as a way to analyse how the cultural transduction unfolds, two concepts were used to group each of these instances: hybridity and convergence. These two terms have been used to describe similar things, although the former has been used in a more general manner than the latter, and there is an association between new forms of cultural exchange, offered by the internet, which underscore the use of the term convergence.

## Hybridity

The term hybridity has been used by a variety of cultural studies academics to describe processes of multicultural exchange (see Bhabha, 1994; García-Canclini, 2004, 2011). The decision to use hybridity to specifically define those processes that take place within formal settings does not necessarily reflect the position of either Bhabha or García-Canclini, but it was a way to disentangle it from the other concept to be used, namely convergence. García-Canclini (1997) has claimed that the term was useful for him to express the different ways in which multicultural contact had become fruitful, and how it has "engendered happy marriages between pre-Columbian iconography and contemporary geometrism, between the visual and musical culture of the elite, pre-massive popular [culture] and that from communication industries"[4] (p. 112). It is the latter point that is highlighted here. Hybridity takes place in all spheres of society, and clearly it is a continuous process of balancing power, economic interests, and political action. The need to limit the value of hybridity to the specific process of media and other established corporations and institutions seeks to overcome the criticism it has received of being tautological by simply referring to the way in which cultural elements are mixed in all processes of interaction (Wang & Yeh, 2005). We concur that "the issue here is not one of finding evidence for hybridization or the equally visible structural imbalances involved, but how hybridization takes place and what it produces" (p. 177).

Hybridity is confined for the purpose of using the concept within cultural transduction to institutional forms of transformation, mainly to try to create it as a distinct category that does not become equivalent to multicultural negotiations. The hybridisation carried out by institutions is a conscious endeavour with its own underlying interests yet acknowledges the importance of modifying something external to satisfy and be affected by the local culture. Obviously, this process could exemplify which elements are retained from dominant cultures, and looking at how hybridity takes place within these institutions helps define the characteristics of the cultural transduction processes and evidences the positions of those involved, who determine what is worth hybridising and how. The case presented here does not seek to use the concept as a "simplified version of hybridity, as fostering the mercantilist domestication of art, making it easier to sell more albums, films and TV shows to other regions"[5] (García Canclini, 2003, p 15), but rather as the scenario for those discussions to arise, by accepting that institutional approaches to cultural transduction are seeking to hybridise precisely with that idea in mind.

Each process of transformation of television formats when they reach a new market is a case of hybridisation of content. There are scores of academic articles dedicated to comparing different versions of format adaptations to understand the underlying cultural nuances that were removed, modified, or extended, including aspects of the aesthetics, development of the narrative for the case of fiction, or other modifications for unscripted formats (see, for instance, Breeden & de Bruin, 2010; Chalaby, 2011, 2016; Moran, 2009, 2006; Nkosi Ndlela, 2013; Pérez-Gómez, 2011, pp. 825–876; Quail, 2015; Ribke, 2022; Shahaf, 2014; Stehling, 2013; Štětka, 2012; to name but a few). There are similar quantities of academic texts focusing on the transformation of films, whether based on films produced originally elsewhere, or those cases that involved the change of medium as well as the change of cultural market (see Cartmell & Whelehan, 1999; Kranz & Mellerski, 2008; Perdikaki, 2018). Remakes are processes of hybridisation by bringing a given story to a different cultural market than the original version of the same product. Video games might be prepared by production and distribution companies to contain sufficient material for consumption elsewhere, including ensuring an appropriate translation of key menus and marketing elements (see Box 5.1) or even aim for adapting all assets, in different levels of localisation (see Bernal Merino, 2016; Fernández Costales, 2012, 2016; Mejías Climent, 2021). The focus here is on the institutionalised processes of generating these

**Box 5.1 Wales Interactive and international game localisation**

Wales Interactive is a video games and interactive movie developer from South Wales in the UK. Their games have received ample recognition, including earning a variety of awards. Their game *Maid of Sker* (2020) has received ample recognition by achieving over a million downloads by 2021 and including a series of Welsh-language songs to accompany the story, set in the Welsh countryside at the end of the 19th century. Its follow-up game, *Sker Ritual* (2022) is currently available in ten language versions including interface elements and subtitles, with audio material offered exclusively in English.

Their approach has been international, and they keep track of how their products perform within a variety of markets through the information they collect from the platforms where they are downloaded, paying attention to those comments they receive. It was clear from early on that they needed to ensure an appropriate translation of all the interactive menus in their games and interactive films. Because of the international nature of platforms, making their contact available in various languages increases the chance of their products being downloaded in other spaces. Language adaptation of their marketing materials exemplifies the type of choices they must make. In the *Sker Ritual* marketing banner in English (see Figure 5.1) and the one in simplified Chinese (see Figure 5.2) are similar, but the placement of the symbol of the bird and the details of the fonts can be spotted to be different. It is not only an issue of language translation, but also of adapting the visual content included to suit a different cultural market.

*Figure 5.1*  Sker Ritual marketing banner for steam in English. Courtesy of Wales Interactive.

*Figure 5.2* Sker Ritual marketing banner for steam in simplified Chinese. Courtesy of Wales Interactive.

modifications, including copyright negotiations, market-bound distribution rights and similar aspects.

Many contemporary debates on the transformation of audiovisual products have made use of the concept of hybridity to describe the process within the confines of films (see the case for *Mulan* in Zhao et al., 2022 and Wang & Yeh, 2005; and *Turning Red* in Chen & Liu, 2023), TV shows (see Neo-orientalist telenovelas in Ribke, 2017; or Malaysian TV shows in Ishak, 2011; and international co-production in McMurria, 2009 and Davis & Nadler, 2010) or other forms of popular culture (see the case of Korean pop music in Shim, 2006 and Kim, 2021), as seen mainly through an institutional lens. Hybridity as a concept seems to be appropriately used in this way to describe cultural transduction that takes place within formal institutions dedicated to media production and distribution, because it highlights how organisations understand their roles as links between two cultural markets through product modification.

## Convergence

The concept of convergence has been used to describe a variety of situations as well, including mergers of media companies, creative changes in media production and the possibilities that fans and other audiences display to create their own media products (Arango-Forero et al., 2016). Here the concept is centred on the latter aspect which has been fundamental to the work of Jenkins (2006; Jenkins et al., 2013) and Deuze (2007). This way of talking about convergence removes other aspects that have been debated with the concept, including the way media systems have become more similar between them in Europe (see Halin & Mancini, 2017) or the use of internet as a distribution channel for a variety of media products (see Larrondo et al., 2012; Cooke, 2005).

Convergence for cultural transduction is concerned with how non-institutional agents develop forms of insertion of cultural products into other cultural markets. Sometimes it is through a process of mediation that includes using online forums and virtual or physical events, practices that include fan-dubbing, fan-subbing, or fan-fiction in general, machinimas, mashups, memes, gifs, and so on. The cultural transduction of *anime* in the US exemplifies convergence through the way fans and interested audiences spread a series of cultural products from a different market through networks of friends and acquaintances, providing their own translations and subtitling (Leonard, 2005; Lee, 2011; Pérez-Gonzalez, 2006). Leonard (2005) has named this situation a cultural sink and defined it as "a void that forms in a culture as a result of intracultural or transcultural flows" (p. 283), when the interest for certain products from another culture or interest group are not readily available within a market. This cultural sink is responsible for the growth of *anime* fan-subbing, and pirate networks of distribution which led to conventions and finally to the re-emergence of authorised formal distribution of Japanese *anime* copyrighted material. Just like fansubs and fandubs for *anime*, non-professional subtitling readily available as soon as series make it to different sharing platforms (Orrego Carmona & Richter, 2018) exemplifies the cultural sink. When there is a gap for this type of product modification or addition, fans and interested consumers find a way to fill the void and promote access to the cultural products they are interested in sharing.

Another contemporary example of convergence culture is the internet meme, which has become ubiquitous and, as pointed out already, have made everyday situations and persons into internationally recognised faces. Shifman (2014) has presented an extensive account of internet memes and provides their description as

(a) a group of digital items sharing common characteristics of content, form, and/or stance, which (b) were created with awareness of each other, and (c) were circulated, imitated, and/or transformed via the Internet by many users.

(p. 41)

Shifman (2014) also provided a differentiation between "viral" and "meme", arguing that "the features that lead us to share a certain video or photo differ from the features that drive us to mimic or remix it" (p. 171). Memes are interesting in our case, rather than virals, because memes are modified and adapted by those who exchange them. They are akin to interchangeable building bricks. They can convey a variety of messages using different elements and remain in an intertextual relation with similar memes. In this recreation and redefinition of meaning that draws upon previous knowledge, they can construct many different types of messages (Trevisan & Goethel, 2015). Memes are not always elements for cultural transduction, for they do not necessarily convey meanings that are drawn from different cultural markets. But most memes do precisely that, by bringing the particular meaning conveyed by some of the elements and placing them in contrast with other elements of particular interest to a given cultural audience (see Box 5.2).

Memes, like any other cultural product, are not necessarily exclusive of convergence. Recently, international corporations have also taken advantage of internet memes and they have become part of the marketing strategies of companies such as Netflix (Puccini-Montoya et al., in press), spinning convergence into hybridity. Therefore, it cannot be said that memes are always convergence, in the same way that audiovisual productions, like films or videos, are not automatically examples of hybridity.

## Cultural transduction labs

As the process of transforming cultural products to suit other cultural interests has become a commercially successful venture, companies have begun to specialise in that area of work, concerned exclusively with the process of transforming cultural products. Cultural transduction labs include dubbing studios, game localisation companies, co-creation platforms, and, sometimes, digital spaces designed for multiple testing. In many of these laboratories there could be a mixture of institutionalised forms of labour with volunteer participation and input. They incorporate both sides of the coin by ensuring there is a simultaneous amount of formal, organised and paid work taking place at the same time as volunteer, unpaid, fan collaboration.

Sometimes it becomes hard to pinpoint specific cultural transduction labs, because they appear to emerge from convergent practices that constantly share, modify and repurpose products in a voluntary way. But some of those spaces have become more than just places to engage with others and transformed, wholly or partially, into enterprises dedicated to transduction which profit from paid and unpaid expertise alike.[6] This includes the case of video game testers, who fall down the crevice of paid and unpaid labour oftentimes

---

**Box 5.2** *Cinderella of the coast* **memes**

The famous image of Cinderella from the eponymous film by Disney has appeared in a variety of memes specifically located in the northern coast of Colombia. The version in most of the memes presents the image of Cinderella in situations that are not very lady-like, including swearing, taking a full bus, or making references to heavy drinking and casual sex. The appeal of the memes relates to the contrast of the gendered expected behaviour of a woman as a "princess", and the way the character of Cinderella behaves in the situations presented. The meme has thousands of reproductions in many different settings and with different juxtapositions of content, from a simple balloon containing an informal dialectal version of Spanish, to a series of images mixed with pictures and balloons.

Although this appropriation only incorporates a subset of all memes based on Cinderella, it brings about a form of cultural transduction in the appropriation of the character and its placement within a clear contextual room of interpretation that at once takes advantage of the renowned characteristics of the Disney princess and their perceived value as representing patriarchal ideas.

You can find a compilation of the memes at https://csar2612.wixsite.com/theothercinderella/galerias-1

Uribe-Jongbloed, E. & Mora-Moreo, C. (2020). The transformation of a Disney princess into its parodic Meme: A case of the cultural transduction of the *Cenicienta Costeña*. In A. Weedon & N. Darwood (Eds.), *Retelling Cinderella: Cultural and creative transformations* (pp. 16–33). Cambridge Scholars.

---

based on considering their job a simple entertainment endeavour (Bulut, 2015a, 2015b).

A similar situation happens with the expansion of webtoons. These sequential art-forms designed to be read by scrolling up on a vertical screen – such as a smartphone – have grown massively in Korea in the 21st century (Cho, 2021). They have been spreading and crossing borders, with platforms that provide a space for collective creation and translation (Nam & Jung, 2022). The website Webtoon Translate is a great repository of webtoons that have been translated into various languages by members of the community as they become available. It shows another aspect of the collaborative convergence culture. It is the concerted efforts of interested actors that provide these cultural transductions. Yecies et al. (2020) present the work of these participants as co-creators as akin to that of the video game localisers and define them as "transcreators" ( p. 53), a term that resembles that of cultural transductor used in this book. They state that

> localizing webtoons, or at least facilitating the crowdsourced creation of multi-language retranslations, has become a key localization strategy, primarily achieved by adapting user translations. This simple but time-consuming process avoids the costs of translating original Korean elements into multiple languages – an important consideration when funding is limited and a mature monetization model for the industry is yet to be developed
>
> (p. 54),

demanding also that the work of those participating in this process should be further recognised.

These types of interactions of co-creative labour sit awkwardly with our common assumptions around paid work, labour and rights, making it clear that

> co-creative relationships in the global cultural economy of the media in-dustries are a significant object of investigation, and that one needs to be aware of both the promises and pitfalls of deploying perspectival frame-works that are grounded in more or less traditional theories of value, mar-kets, and labour.
>
> (Banks & Deuze, 2009, p. 425)

These new debates spark up about what has been dubbed the "gig econ-omy", "an increasingly common employment relationship in which the risks of both labor and capital are displaced onto individual workers" (Curtin & Sanson, 2017, p. 28), and clearly a subset of the practices that arise thanks to the technological advances, exchange possibilities and the expansion of the convergence culture (Jenkins, 2006). These spaces of co-creative labour might turn into systems of exploitation of creativity, a diluted recognition of authorship and unpaid work predicated upon the pleasure to participate in a creative industry where your passion is the driving force (see Chia, 2019). They are also great sites of transcultural exchange, expanding and helping the diffusion of other types of cultural products.

## Studying the social structures of the phenomenon

Cultural transduction, as has been seen thus far, takes place in physical and virtual settings, it includes economic interests of national and transna-tional corporations aiming to exploit cross-cultural predictability, reducing cultural distance, and diminishing costs in the production of new ideas by exploring some that have already been tested and have rendered profits (see Chapters 2 and 3). On the other hand, people voluntarily offer their knowledge, skills, and expertise to transform cultural products with the interest of gaining recognition, sharing personal tastes, or engaging in communities of interest.

The human factor on the decision for the transduction of products is key for the institutional or corporate interests as well as for fan-based engagement (see Chapter 4). These mechanics allow for more cultural products to travel and receive engagement beyond their original point of conception. As has already been debated, some of these products might even be directly designed or elaborated with a larger market in mind from the onset. As the site of these processes, studying where the transduction process is carried out helps to understand why some products travel while others do not. It brings to light the steps that products take in their transformation, the interests behind the adaptation, the procedures they undergo, and the relation they have with working conditions, financial decisions, and social appreciation of cultural labour (see Miller, 2020; Curtin & Sanson, 2016, 2017). It also highlights the various forms of cultural exchange and appropriation that might take place within institutional and non-institutional settings, which tells us about intellectual property development, cultural appropriation, gendered practices (see Duffy, 2016; Harvey & Shepherd, 2017), copyright (see Phillips & Street, 2015), and exploitation (see Fuchs, 2018).

It is impossible to cover all potential aspects that would benefit from analysing the processes through which cultural products are selected, modified, and inserted into other cultural markets. However, through the use of the process tenet of the cultural transduction framework, the idea is that these elements are brought to light and assessed to understand the decisions made, the strategies developed for insertion, and the paths that have been adopted for that insertion to take place.

## Notes

1 This video can be seen here: https://www.youtube.com/watch?v=eQrJqhm-gcc
2 This version of the video is available here: https://www.youtube.com/watch?v=lj7lQDeBNll
3 The story of András Arató in the "Hide the pain Harold" meme has been told many times (see, for instance, Arató, 2019; Mag, 2019), as well as Denise Sánchez "Girl explaining" meme sudden rise to fame (Paúl, 2022) to highlight only two.
4 Translation by the author from the original in Spanish.
5 Translation by the author from the original in Spanish.
6 Consider the case of Little Big Planet (LBP) a space created by Media Molecule and published by Sony Computer Entertainment, as a site where players can create their own content for other players to engage with (Comunello & Mulargia, 2015).

64 *The process tenet*

## References

Arango-Forero, G., Roncallo-Dow, S., & Uribe Jongbloed, E. (2016). Rethinking media convergence. In A. Lugmary & C. Dal Zotto (Eds.), *Media convergence handbook. Journalism, broadcasting, and social media aspects of convergence* (pp. 17–28). Springer-Verlag Berlin Heidelberg. https://doi.org/10.1007/978-3-642-54484-2_2

Arató, A. (2019, Nov. 8). Experience: My face became a meme. *The Guardian.* https://www.theguardian.com/lifeandstyle/2019/nov/08/experience-hide-the-pain-harold-face-became-meme-turned-it-into-career

Banks, J., & Deuze, M. (2009). Co-creative labour. *International Journal of Cultural Studies, 12*(5), 419–431. https://doi.org/10.1177/1367877909337862

Bernal Merino, M. Á. (2016). Glocalization and co-creation. Trends in international game production. In A. Esser, M. Á. Bernal Merino, & I. R. Smith (Eds.), *Media across borders. localizing TV, films and video games* (pp. 202–220). Routledge.

Bhabha, H. K. (1994). *The location of culture.* Routledge.

Bulut, E. (2015a). Glamor above, precarity below: Immaterial labour in the video game industry. *Critical Studies in Media Communication, 32*(3), 193–207. Https://doi.org/10.1080/15295036.2015.1047880

Bulut, E. (2015b). Playboring in the tester pit: The convergence of precarity and the degradation of fun in video game testing. *Television & New Media, 16*(3), 240–258. https://doi.org/10.1177/1527476414525241

Breeden, A., & De Bruin, J. (2010). The office: Articulations of national identity in television format adaptation. *Television & New Media, 11*(1), 3–19.

Cartmell, D., & Whelehan, I. (Eds.). (1999). *Adaptations: From text to screen, screen to text.* Routledge.

Chalaby, J. K. (2016). Drama without drama: The late rise of scripted TV formats. *Television & New Media, 17*(1), 3–20. https://doi.org/10.1177/1527476414561089

Chalaby, J. K. (2011). The making of an entertainment revolution: How the TV format trade became a global industry. *European Journal of Communication, 26*(4), 293–309. https://doi.org/10.1177/0267323111423414

Chen, R. & Liu, Y. (2023) A study on Chinese audience's receptive behavior towards Chinese and western cultural hybridity films based on grounded theory—Taking Disney's animated film turning red as an example. *Behavioral Science, 13*, 135. https://doi.org/10.3390/bs13020135

Chia, A. (2019). The moral calculus of vocational passion in digital gaming. *Television & New Media, 20*(8), 767–777. https://doi.org/10.1177/15274764198510

Cho, H. (2021). The platformization of culture: Webtoon platforms and media ecology in Korea and beyond. *Journal of Asian Studies, 80*(1), 73–93. doi: https://doi.org/10.1017/S0021911820002405

Comunello, F., & Mulargia, S. (2015). User-generated video gaming: Little big planet and participatory cultures in Italy. *Games and Culture, 10*(1), 57–80. https://doi.org/10.1177/1555412014557028

Cooke, L. (2005). A visual convergence of print, television, and the internet: Charting 40 years of design change in news presentation. *New Media & Society, 7*(1), 22–46. https://doi.org/10.1177/1461444805049141

Curtin, M., & Sanson, K. (2017). Listening to labor. In M. Curtin & K. Sanson (Eds.), *Voices of labor* (pp. 1–17). University of California Press.

Curtin, M., & Sanson, K. (2016). Precarious creativity: Global media, local labor. In M. Curtin & K. Sanson (Eds.), *Precarious creativity* (pp. 1–18). University of California Press.

Davis, C. H., & Nadler, J. (2010). International television co-productions and the cultural discount: The case of family biz, a comedy. *9th World Media Management and Economics Conference*. http://www.ryerson.ca/~c5davis/publications/Nadler-Davis-InternationalTelevisionCoproductionv7-12May2010.pdf

Deuze, M. (2007). Convergence culture in the creative industries. *International Journal of Cultural Studies, 10*(2), 243–263. https://doi.org/10.1177/1367877907076793

Duffy, B. E. (2016). The romance of work: Gender and aspirational labour in the digital culture industries. *International Journal of Cultural Studies, 19*(4), 441–457. https://doi.org/10.1177/1367877915572186

Fernández Costales, A. (2016). Analyzing players' perceptions on the translation of video games. In A. Esser, M. Á. Bernal-Merino, & I. R. Smith (Eds.), *Media across borders: Localizing TV, film, and video games* (pp. 183–201). Routledge.

Fernández Costales, A. (2012). Exploring translation strategies in Video Game localisaton. *Monografías de Traducción e Interpretación, 4*, 385–408. https://doi.org/10.6035/MonTI.2014.4.16

Fuchs, C. (2018). Capitalism, patriarchy, slavery, and racism in the age of digital capitalism and digital labour. *Critical Sociology, 44*(4–5), 677–702. https://doi.org/10.1177/0896920517691108

García-Canclini, N. (1997). Culturas hibridas y estrategias comunicacionales. *Estudios sobre las culturas contemporáneas, 3*(5), 109–128.

García-Canclini, N. (2003). Noticias recientes sobre la hibridación. *Trans. Revista Transcultural de Música, 7*, 1–17.

García-Canclini, N. (2004). *Diferentes, desiguales y desconectados*. Gedisa.

García-Canclini, N. (2011). *Culturas Híbridas: Estrategias para entrar y salir de la modernidad*. Debolsillo.

Hallin, D. C. & Mancini, P. (2017). Ten years after comparing media systems: What have we learned? *Political Communication, 34*(2), 155–171. Https://doi.org/10.108 0/10584609.2016.1233158

Harvey, A., & Shepherd, T. (2017). When passion isn't enough: gender, affect and credibility in digital games design. *International Journal of Cultural Studies, 20*(5), 492–508. https://doi.org/10.1177/1367877916636140

Ishak, S. Z. A. (2011). Cultural hybridity: Adapting and filtering popular culture in Malaysian television programmes. *Jurnal Pengajian Media Malaysia - Malaysian Journal of Media studies, 13*(1), 1–15

Jenkins, H. (2006). *Convergence culture: Where old and new media collide*. New York University Press.

Jenkins, H., Ford, S., & Green, J. (2013). *Spreadable media: Creating value and meaning in a network culture*. New York University Press.

Johnson, M. R. (2017). The use of ASCII graphics in roguelikes: Aesthetic nostalgia and semiotic difference. *Games and Culture, 12*(2), 115–135. https://doi.org/10.1177/1555412015585884

Kim, J. O. (2021). The Korean wave and the new global media economy. In D.Y. Jin (Ed.), *The Routledge handbook of digital media and globalization* (pp. 77–85). Routledge.

Kranz, D. L. & Mellerski, N. C. (Eds.). (2008). *In/fidelity: Essays on film adaptation*. Cambridge Scholars Publishing.

Larrondo, A., Larrañaga, J., Meso, K. & Agirreazkuenaga, I. (2012). The convergence process in public audiovisual groups. *Journalism Practice, 6*(5–6), 788–797, Https://doi.org/10.1080/17512786.2012.667282

66    *The process tenet*

Lee, H.-K. (2011). Participatory media fandom: A case study of anime fansubbing. *Media, Culture & Society, 33*(8), 1131–1147. https://doi.org/10.1177/0163443711418271

Leonard, S. (2005). Progress against the law: Anime and fandom, with the key to the globalization of culture. *International Journal of Cultural Studies, 8*(3), 281–305. https://doi.org/10.1177/1367877905055679

Mag. (2019, Nov. 27). La curiosa historia de András Arató, el hombre detrás del famoso meme 'Hide the pain, Harold'. *El Comercio.* https://mag.elcomercio.pe/historias/hide-the-pain-harold-andras-aratos-meme-historia-nnda-nnrt-chile-espana-mexico-colombia-argentina-video-fotos-noticia/

McMurria, J. (2009). Moby dick, cultural policy and the geographies and geopolitics of cultural labor. *International Journal of Cultural Studies, 12*(3), 237–256. https://doi.org/10.1177/1367877908101570

Mejías-Climent, L. (2021). *Enhancing video game localization through dubbing.* Routledge.

Melo Sarmiento, G. (2020). La parodia: Reflexión y elementos propuestos para su interpretación en Colombia. *Revista La Propiedad Inmaterial, 29,* 215–239.

Miller, T. (2020). *El trabajo cultural.* Gedisa.

Moran, A. (ed.) (2009). *TV formats worldwide. Localizing global programs.* Intellect.

Moran, K. C. (2006). The global expansion of children's television: A case study of the adaptation of Sesame Street in Spain. *Learning, Media and Technology, 31*(3), 287–300. https://doi.org/10.1080/17439880600893333

Nam, J., & Jung, Y. (2022). Exploring fans' participation in digital media: Transcreation of webtoons. *Telecommunications Policy, 46,* 1–14. https://doi.org/10.1016/j.telpol.2022.102407

Nkosi Ndlela, M. (2013). Television across boundaries: Localisation of big brother Africa. *Critical Studies in Television: An International Journal of Television Studies, 8*(2), 57–72. https://doi.org/10.7227/CST.8.2.6

Orrego-Carmona, D. & Richter, S. (2018). Tracking distribution of non-professional subtitles to study new audiences. *Observatorio, 2,* 64–86.

Paúl, M. L. (2022, Aug. 22). How a photo of a woman yelling in a guy's ear became a viral meme. *Washington Post.* https://www.washingtonpost.com/nation/2022/08/22/girl-explaining-meme-twitter-viral/

Perdikaki, K. (2018). Film adaptation as the interface between creative translation and cultural transformation: The case of Baz Luhrmann's the great gatsby. *The Journal of Specialised Translation, 29,* 169–187.

Pérez-Gómez, M. (Ed.) (2011). *Previously on.* Universidad de Salamanca.

Pérez-González, L. (2006). Fansubbing Anime: Insights into the "butterfly effect" of globalization in audiovisual translation. *Perspectives: Studies in Translatology, 14*(4), 260–277.

Phillips, T., & Street, J. (2015). Copyright and musicians at the digital margins. *Media, Culture & Society, 37*(3), 342–358. https://doi.org/10.1177/0163443714567018

Puccini-Montoya, A., Mora-Moreo, C. & Uribe-Jongbloed, E. (In press). Local memes, global production: Cultural transduction in the Netflix promotion strategy in Colombia. In L. Popa, R. Groots & S. Lavie (Eds.), *Cultural identities in a global world: Reframing cultural hybridity.* GCSC.

Quail, C. (2015). Anatomy of a format: So you think you can dance Canada and discourses of commercial nationalism. *Television & New Media, 16*(5), 472–489. https://doi.org/10.1177/1527476414543527

Ribke, N. (2022). Bilingual fiction series, genre conventions, and the economy of linguistic interaction in Israeli television. *International Journal of Cultural Studies*, *25*(6), 673–689. https://doi.org/10.1177/13678779221114380

Ribke, N. (2017). Media imperialism beyond the Anglo-Saxon axis, or negotiated hybridity? Neo-Orientalist telenovelas and transnational business in Brazilian television. *Journal of Consumer Culture*, *17*(3), 562–578. https://doi.org/10.1177/1469540515602303

Roncallo-Dow, S. (2016). Confused Travolta o el placer de lo simple. *Palabra Clave – Revista de Comunicación*, *19*(1), 8–14. https://doi.org/10.5294/pacla.2016.19.1.1

Scolari, C.A., Bertetti, P. & Freeman, M. (2014). *Transmedia archaeology: Storytelling in the borderlines of science fiction, comics and pulp magazines*. Palgrave Pivot.

Shahaf, S. (2014). Homegrown reality: Locally formatted Israeli programming and the global spread of format TV. *Creative Industries Journal*, *7*(1), 3–18. https://doi.org/10.1080/17510694.2014.892264

Shim, D. (2006). Hybridity and the rise of Korean popular culture in Asia. *Media, Culture & Society*, *28*(1), 25–44. https://doi.org/10.1177/0163443706059278

Shifman, L. (2014). *Memes in digital culture*. MIT Press.

Stehling, M. (2013). From localisation to translocalisation: Audience readings of the television format top model. *Critical Studies in Television*, *8*(2), 36–53.

Štětka, V. (2012). From global to (g)local: Changing patterns of television program flows and audience preferences in Central and Eastern Europe. *Journal of Popular Film and Television*, *40*(3), 109–118. https://doi.org/10.1080/01956051.2012.697779

Szwydky, L. L. (2023). CODA: Transmedia cultural history, convergence culture and the future of adaptation studies. In L.L. Szwydky & G. Jellenik (Eds.), *Adaptation before cinema: Literary and visual convergence from antiquity through the nineteenth century* (pp. 283–303). PalgraveMacmillan. https://doi.org/10.1007/978-3-031-09596-2_13

Thomas, A. O. (2006). Cultural economics of TV programme cloning: Or why India has produced multi-"millionaires." *International Journal of Emerging Markets*, *1*(1), 35–47. https://doi.org/10.1108/17468800610644997

Trevisan, M. K., & Goethel, M. F. (2015). Meme: Intertextualidades e apropriações na Internet. *Revista Observatório*, *2*(1), 277–298. https://doi.org/10.20873/uft.2447-4266.2016v2n1p277

Uribe-Jongbloed, E., Barker, K. & Scholz, T. (2021). Lecciones europeas sobre el copyright en línea: ¿una advertencia para América Latina sobre la parodia, los memes y la expresión creativa? [European lessons on copyright: A note of warning for Latin America on parody, memes and creative expression?]. In *Consideraciones sobre el Derecho de Autor en el Entorno de Internet en América Latina* (pp. 107–119). Universidad de San Andrés & CETyS. https://cetys.lat/wp-content/uploads/2021/04/Compilado.pdf

Uribe-Jongbloed, E. & Mora-Moreo, C. (2020). The transformation of a Disney princess into its parodic Meme: A case of the cultural transduction of the *Cenicienta Costeña*. In A. Weedon & N. Darwood (Eds.), *Retelling Cinderella: Cultural and creative transformations* (pp. 16–33). Cambridge Scholars.

Uribe-Jongbloed, E., & Roncallo-Dow, S. (2018). Stranger things and our memories of Colombian TV in the late eighties. Bringing back ALF, V.I.C.I., Evie and Guri-Guri.

In K. J. Wetmore (Ed.), *Uncovering stranger things. Essays on eighties nostalgia, cynicism and innocence in the series* (pp. 49–59). McFarland & Company.

Wang, G., & Yeh, E. Y. (2005). Globalization and hybridization in cultural products: The cases of Mulan and Crouching Tiger, Hidden Dragon. *International Journal of Cultural Studies, 8*(2), 175–193. https://doi.org/10.1177/1367877905052416

Weedon, A. (2021). *The origins of transmedia storytelling in early twentieth century adaptation.* Palgrave Macmillan.

Yecies, B., Shim, A., Yang, J., & Zhong, P. Y. (2020). Global transcreators and the extension of the Korean webtoon IP-engine. *Media, Culture and Society, 42*(1), 40–57. https://doi.org/10.1177/0163443719867277

Zhao, M., Ang, L. H., & Toh, F.H.C. (2022). Hybridising the cultural identity of Mulan from a Chinese ballad to American films. *Asian Journal of Social Science, 50*(2), 130–136. https://doi.org/10.1016/j.ajss.2021.10.001

# 6 Guidelines for cultural transduction in product development and trade

## Analysing instances of cultural transduction

It has already been mentioned that this approach comes from trying to bring together already established areas of study that have achieved recognition in their own right and that have begun to discuss the same issues from different but usually complementary perspectives. Media studies, drawing from the traditional critical perspectives of the Frankfurt school, has taken a political economy approach that is very useful to study markets and how they work and enable or constrain cultural transduction (see Miller et al., 2005; Miller & Yúdice, 2004; Bolaño, 2012). Media economics has also been interested in this aspect, as it recognises the important contribution that all forms of media have on economic output, and looks at mergers, collaboration, and coproduction in media sectors, as well as emerging business strategies and developments (for instance, Rohn, 2004, 2010). From adaptation studies, including those that come from screenwriting and literary studies, we have found an overall interest in media characteristics that transfer well between different media renditions or other details that are often linked to the transfer of content between similar or dissimilar media (see Hutcheon, 2013; Elliot, 2013; Sanders, 2006; Sherry, 2016; Szwydky, 2023). Even the cases that are presented here, which tend to be more ample than the ones often present in adaptation studies, are but a fraction of all the forms of exchange of characteristics between dissimilar media, as Elleström (2017a, 2017b) has pointed out. There is also influence from areas of media studies including games, TV formats and digital media studies, to address aspects of the products that travel or fail to do so, between cultural spaces. Linguistics and translation studies have also provided ample developments in this field, and the similitude between cultural transduction and cultural translation has to do with precisely this situation; coming from different angles, there is common ground to explore in the middle.

The addition of the people within the cultural transduction framework might be one of the aspects that is often overlooked by other areas of study. It does not mean that the aspects of the individuals involved in these processes have not been addressed – they have been considered as informants

DOI: 10.4324/9781003380221-6

in countless research projects based on interviews – but rather that they are presented here under a different conceptual light. Obviously, it does not align one to one with the way companies advertise or give names to the roles involved (García Avis y Diego, 2018), but it provides a useful shorthand for describing what people working in these processes do (see Cuelenaere, 2020). The focus on the people engaged has been relevant to the growing field of cultural translation, because the role of the translator as creator, rather than just as a cog in a machine, has become one of their central debates.

Finally, thinking about the companies, organisations, and voluntary associations where these processes ensue has also been something that has become of interest from media studies, again in their more critical or managerial side, or from those concerned with audience studies and fan participation. Audiovisual translation studies, which also sits comfortably between media studies, linguistics, modern languages and translation studies, has provided a good amount of work that is relevant in this part of the framework.

The four tenets (see Table 6.1) of the cultural transduction framework lend themselves to be applied for the analysis of the travels of media and cultural products in a variety of ways.

### Focusing on one of the tenets

One way to take advantage of the cultural transduction framework is to concentrate on each tenet separately as an individual area of exploration.

For all sorts of purposes, it would be useful to focus solely on the market relations between two or more cultural markets. These could be nations, in the case of broadcasting or media regulations, copyright or trade agreements in the media sector, or they could be subsets of national markets, like those in

*Table 6.1* The complete cultural transduction framework

| Market | Product | People | Process |
|---|---|---|---|
| Cultural proximity/ distance | Shareability/ transparency | Scout | Hybridity |
| | Cultural lacunae | Merchant | Convergence |
| Cultural barriers | • Content | Alchemist | Cultural transduction |
| Cross-cultural predictability | • Capital | Jack-of-all-trades | lab |
| | • Production | | |
| Cultural tolerance | Cultural universals | | |
| | • Content | | |
| | • Audience-created | | |
| | • Company-created | | |
| | Discourse proximity | | |
| | Cultural discount | | |

minority language settings, or regions in the case of diaspora or migrant communities, geolinguistic markets, or transnational gaming groups. Studying the relationship between close or distant markets regarding their cultural barriers, or the cultural predictability of their market successes, is something worth exploring in its own right.

A singular analysis on the product tenet might focus on one product or a series of them and its characteristics to succeed in other markets. This type of assessment is particularly useful for those interested in determining the likelihood of product transposition. In this case, an analysis of cultural lacunae and universals would inform the best insertion or trade strategy. It could also be used to undertake a comparison between the different forms developed by those products that have been transducted to understand the cultural differences highlighted by the way the product has been developed elsewhere and what it tells us in terms of discourse proximity and cultural discount. Perhaps is this the tenet under which most works have already been undertaken, since both adaptation and translation studies have paid great attention to how these changes have come to be in a great variety of products throughout history.

Analysis devoted to the people tenet provides recognition of the impact of individual decisions in the travels of audiovisual products. Despite many products having potential traits that would render them suitable for travel without a passport, only a fraction of them cross borders. Film studies, for instance, has dedicated years to studying individual authors and creators who have made products available in other markets based on their own creative genius or stubbornness. This tenet would benefit from understanding more profoundly how people involved in transduction processes understand their role as intermediaries. Both their lived experiences and incorporated shorthand tell us about how they understand cultural markets and specific products. In the case of alchemists who undertake the insertion of the product to a market, their decisions highlight how they understand their target audience, what expectations they have, and what they make of their role as keepers and creators of cultural taste.

It is also interesting to understand more about how old and new associations, organisations, and corporations are dedicating themselves to these processes of bringing material across borders. The internal motivations, structures, working practices, and conditions become particularly interesting in the digital era, "gig economy" and age of convergence which include self-employment, self-fulfilment, and, as Byung-Chul Han (2015) has warned, self-exploitation. Looking at hybridity or convergence does not imply a mindless praise for all cultural transpositions, but rather a reflexive stance that may also include debates about cultural appropriation, exoticisation, and extraction. Looking at broadcasters, platforms, brands, and interest groups to comprehend their procedures, motivations, and monetisation strategies in cultural transduction would allow a more nuanced approach to discussions about labour, multicultural exchange, author's rights, and cultural diversity.

The emphasis here is placed on the underlying assumptions and practices that make up global media exchanges.

The framework is not limited by each of the tenets as a space to be analysed independently, since a more complex picture could arise from studies across its horizontal axis, looking at more than one tenet at a time.

### *Cultural transduction across tenets*

The framework lends itself to be used as a series of aspects to be studied when looking at specific case studies or scenarios. Any process of multiple iterations, as could be the case of multiple adaptations of a series of books to a film spanning over longer periods, could be studied using the framework, addressing the transmedia cultural history of a product, for instance (see Szwydky, 2023). Even by taking one single example, going through each of the tenets provides a more holistic perspective than being limited by what each tenet has to offer. Murray (2008) recommended for adaptation studies to embrace its industrial aspects, and to draw from a variety of academic sources to overcome the methodological limitations of textual analysis. Despite criticism regarding the unexplored aspects of literature and film adaptation studies that the model had until that moment (Cattrysse, 2017, 2020), Cattrysse (2017) also valued this potential for the cultural transduction framework.

There is also potential to use this framework from a postcolonial perspective that does not centre its appreciation exclusively on Euro-American parameters. To be postcolonial, in this sense, would imply to avoid the commonplace practice of only addressing cases that are presented as important or relevant in the international market in relation to the largest media market players, and responding to other market sizes, other flows of products and less explored media interactions. Not everything needs to be set in relation to the American or European market interests, but rather more important to understand aspects that cut across other axes and flows. Exploring regional exchanges, products that have travelled through peripheral or small markets, people engaged with local imports from neighbouring countries, or the development of niche interest groups for particular products through platforms, would enhance our understanding of cultural transduction.

### Prospective use of the cultural transduction framework

Another way of looking at the framework is to consider it as a strategic tool for planning insertion of products into a different cultural market. Using the tenets serves as a series of debates that help rendering cultural products easier to modify or adapt to their different expected setting. As presented by Bernal Merino (2016) for the case of video games, there can be a proactive attitude to

product insertion into a market, bearing in mind the needs for cultural transduction from the onset of the product design rather than as a response to ex-
pansive trajectories. As Gerson da Silva, the game designer for *Iron Marines,*
has mentioned (see Box 6.1), to find the way into a specific market requires a
very nuanced understanding of its cultural sensibilities and business processes
to determine the inclusion of suitable material that would increase the appeal
rather than generate rejection because of a lack of attention to a given asset.

---

**Box 6.1 *Iron Marines* and its cultural transduction
process**

Gerson da Silva was the lead game designer of *Iron Marines* (2017) a
video game of Ironhide Game Studio. After the initial success of *Kingdom Rush* (see Box 3.2), and with the interest of developing another
type of game that kept the aesthetics, format, platform, and playability
of their previous success (taking advantage of company-created universals he opted to develop a new game, this time as a strategy game.
The setting was a sci-fi world colonisation and territory-control game.
Sci-fi was selected for its narrative transparency and he opted to keep
the seeming invisibility of the origin of the game (both important for
content universality). He kept English as the main language for in-
game audio files, while the menus and other texts were made available
in ten languages, although not all at the point of inception. Bahasa
Indonesia was added as a way to improve access to the Indonesian
market, but it was included a couple of months after the launch, and
this seemed to have limited its impact.

Conscious decisions were debated with the team regarding the
translation of character names. It was considered that the names would
remain constant regarding the language, to prevent difficulties for
the players to find information on the characters from wherever they
would play them. For instance, *Trabuco* would not be translated into
English as Blunderbuss – keeping the name in Spanish as an Easter
egg for those who speak the language – nor would the character named
Fate be called *Destino* in its Spanish language version. Financial considerations led them to opt out of doing dubbing into other languages,
keeping the audio elements solely in English. Also, direct discussion
with the translators subcontracted was made to ensure that the jokes
in the texts that would not easily translate into another language were
then just kept in their informational value, rather than trying to recreate
the humour.

*Figure 6.1* In-game character of Guiying. Courtesy Inrohide Game Studio

They made a concerted effort in the case of creating the character of Guiying (Figure 6.1). With the explicit interest of developing a character for the Chinese market and reducing cultural discount, they engaged in conversation with their localisation partner in China to ensure that the development of the character would not generate rejection for a stereotypical version. Da Silva mentions that their original research led them to want to create a character called [Wang] Paifeng who they thought was a female descendant of a line of generals who defended the emperor. But when they mentioned this character to their Chinese partner, they considered that the role of Paifeng on the Generals of the Yang Family saga was only a secondary one, and that it would be better to refer to [Mu] Guiying, who has a more prominent role and who is a symbol of a dedicated and strong woman. Furthermore, they mentioned that the character of Guiying had appeared in recent television shows, so it was a character more people were familiar with. After accepting this advice, da Silva mentions that they created some drafts for the character art and send them over to be revised. They had already selected which one they thought was the best one, but they included other discarded sketches as well just in case. Their Chinese partner mentioned that it was fortunate that they had not selected any of the discarded sketches, because those had Guiying with a strand of hair flowing directly in front of her face, and that from the Chinese perspective it would be considered wrong, because that unkempt characteristic was not associated with the Song Dynasty that Guiying was a part of, but rather their barbaric northern enemies. Da Silva then proceeded to generate further images of the character, including its power related to summoning an Eastern Dragon (Figure 6.2).

*Figure 6.2* Guiying hero profile image. Courtesy Ironhide Game Studio.

The Chinese and Korean markets were considered the fundamental ones to tap into, because of their size in number of gamers, and translated versions of the menus were considered important from an early stage. Keeping track of the debates in their own forums and, later, in the ones developed in discord to include their participating audience and gauge their impact, served to improve relatability through audience-created universals and taking advantage of voluntary beta-testing.

The prospective use of the framework may start with recognising market differences, reviewing the product that is being developed to realise its potential in the use of universals and its possible drawbacks from culturally dependent knowledge, determining the best way to establish a transduction, selecting the channels of the development, the people involved in the process, and finally opting for an internal development, an external collaboration or consultancy, or seeking support through convergent channels, including fans.

### Questions to address cultural transduction

Each of the tenets of the framework lends itself to generating a simple questionnaire that might be useful for understanding how to develop the transduction of a product. It serves to also define what is likely to be the best approach at undertaking the cultural transduction, from basic to complex modifications. The set of questions are presented here just as a guideline, they might not all apply to every type of transduction process, but they are useful to bear in mind.

## Market tenet

The objective when analysing the market tenet is to determine cultural proximity, assess cross-cultural predictability, map out market barriers and understand cultural tolerance between the intended markets.

1 What similar characteristics does the intended market share with the source market?
   This question looks at the established relationship between the markets in terms of the language used in media or cultural production, historical links or trade agreements between the markets of the type of product that concerns the analysis.
2 What are the main barriers of access to the market?
   This question looks at the barriers that may exist in terms of levies, quotas, cultural or content demands, restrictions, or limitations.
3 What are known or evident cultural barriers to entry in the market?
   If there are any know examples of trade of cultural products between the markets, it is important to know if they have been well received in the past. Finding information about cultural or religious mores and values of the target market is important to gauge possible entry.
4 How have previous successful products in the source market performed in the destination market?
   Here it is useful to know if there have been products that have already succeeded in entering the market and how well were they received, to assess cross-cultural predictability.
5 Is there an established exchange of any type of cultural products between the markets?
   It is important to know if there are structures of exchange already in place, and if there are bilateral, or multilateral agreements already established between the markets in the products that hope to be inserted.
6 Is there any form of resistance or avoidance of products between the markets?
   If any specific case has popped up regarding a product or types of product that have been negatively perceived or which did not receive entry into the market, its example could prevent further problems.
7 What is the market of origin of other products that have fared positively in the destination market?
   It may be the case that the target market is considerably different from the source market, but products from a similar market to the market of origin have already received entry in the target market, implying there could be cultural tolerance to these types of products from similar markets.
8 How are products from the source market perceived or recognised in the destination market?

It is useful to know if there is already a positive or negative appreciation for products from the source market, even in media that are different from the one you would be interested in participating. These appreciations may serve to determine cultural tolerance.

## Product tenet

The specific product that has been developed or is being developed is evaluated to recognise its potential for crossing markets.

1  How much does the product rely on specific cultural references (e.g. local places, traditions, customs or religious traits)?
   The idea is to recognise the level of cultural dependency of the product, or how to diminish its cultural lacunae before trying to offer it elsewhere.
2  What type of genre would the product be considered to be? (Humour is more difficult to understand in different cultures than fantasy tropes).
   The genre of the product is fundamental because certain genres are more anchored in specific cultural characteristics than others. Although cultural anchoring might not prevent a product from travelling, it requires for the target audience to be familiar with the type of cultural capital required or have ways to overcome it via audience- or company-created universals.
3  Do people in the target market appreciate or engage with that type of product? (It may also be there is a gap in the offer and that is what you seek to fill.)
   Audiences or consumers may already be engaging with similar products through online communities or fan groups. It is important to know if there is already a potential consumer base.
4  Are aspects of the product universal in appeal?
   It may be difficult to gauge how universal the product is but there are some general aspects that are easy to recognise, including the level of complexity of the language used, the commonality of the type of narrative and the main themes of family, love and self-fulfilment. Since universality between markets rests on cultural proximity, it is easier to assess in the context of similar markets.
5  What are potential difficulties in the characteristics of the product that might not lend it to be understood elsewhere? (Think about intertextual references, for instance, and how central they are for the product enjoyment.)
   After looking at potential lacunae, there needs to be an assessment of the relevance of references in the text to other products, places or material. When intertextual recognition is fundamental for product appreciation, for instance in the case of parodies, it becomes very important to know how familiar the target audience is to those intertextual elements.

6   How are the roles depicted and how are they perceived in the receiving culture? (Sensitivity towards certain social roles, names, social strata, might be worth assessing.)
Each culture deals differently with social roles and this may prompt their acceptance or rejection of media products. Proper nouns and names are sometimes modified according to tradition (for instance, most European languages translate some of the names into their local versions), although there is a push towards keeping them in their original form. An assessment of the roles present in the product and the most recent social views on the target market are useful to see in how far thus the product need to be modified to suit local taste and sensitivities.

7   Does the product have traits that are similar to those that are part of established brands, recognisable works or platforms? (Is your product similar to a BBC documentary or an animation akin to Japanese *anime*.)
Here it is useful to assess if there are company-created universals that your product might take advantage of. Even in cases when the product might be considerably different in content or style to a company-created universal, knowing how close it sits to some of its characteristics may simplify adaptation processes.

8   Are elements of the content potentially offensive or controversial in the target market? (Attitudes to sex and violence, for example.)
Sometimes the only people who can assess potential offensiveness are those well versed in the target market, whether because they have a lengthy exposure to it or because they have already participated in trade locally. Local consultants might be the best way to assess this potential cultural discount.

9   Which rights (services or assets) are used or acquired, how and for how long are they to be used? (Format bibles or optioning rights, for instance.)
Different products are traded and exchanged in patterns that have been established for some time. Although there is always room to innovate, it is fundamental to know how have products, like the one being analysed, been traded in the past.

**People tenet**

It is important to think about how your product would be brought to the attention of others or how do you expect to generate interest in it. Deciding what your role would be in the process or who you will engage for it is also fundamental.

1   What role are you playing in the transduction process? (Are you scouting for products, are you selling or buying them or are you in charge of modifying them?)

It is not to be expected that a person will engage with all the roles in the transduction, but you have to know which is the one you are expected to perform.

2  Who would be the delegate for each of the roles?
   If you are playing only a part in the process, it becomes relevant to know who the others are.

3  Do you have the inhouse or personal capacity to carry out the role?
   Knowing the limits of your knowledge and expertise is key to determining whether to undertake a transduction and how best to do it.

4  Who is assessing the characteristics of the product?
   In the case of trade fairs, people are interested in some characteristics and conditions more than others. They will be trying to determine cross-cultural predictability, for instance. In cases where there is no previous success of the product, people might be more concerned with the research behind it and your own commitment to the product.

5  What is the expertise required to assess the product beyond your own abilities?
   You do not always hold the key to knowing if a product will travel well. But you should know who does or try to find out who might do.

6  What elements of the product would need to be modified?
   If you are assessing a product and you can soon notice it has potential but requires modifications, your assessment of the modifications will have an impact on the expected cultural discount. The level and type of modification will determine the best way to acquire, license or distribute the product.

7  What type of modification is required?
   It goes hand in hand with the previous question and it would have financial implications.

8  How has the success in the source market been determined (if at all)?
   If there are ways to assess cross-cultural predictability, it is always a bit of information that any merchant will appreciate.

9  Who would need to be engaged for the modifications or alterations of the product?
   You have to ask yourself if you, or your own company, are capable of undertaking the modifications of the product, if you will require the assistance of a local consultant or one from the product's creators, or if you will find a third party to do it for you.

10 What is the likely cultural discount facing the product?
   This is the main question you will have to wonder when assessing a product from a different cultural market.

## Process tenet

It is relevant to understand the mechanics and spaces where the product will be inserted. This includes knowing about the structure and organisation of the institution or distribution channel and the policies, written and unwritten, that define that space.

1.  Has the institution or organisation undertaken these processes before?
    Previous experience in the business is clearly an asset. In cases of localisation or adaptation, previous successes are often predictors of future success.
2   What is the distribution of the tasks?
    Whether in big companies or small enterprises, the tasks should be clearly defined to ensure that the process is carried out correctly. When some of these tasks are given to third parties or require approval by the providers of the products, these need to be set from the beginning.
3   What are the required steps, participation techniques, support, assets that need to be prepared?
    This is usually the reason why the format bibles and consultant services are so important. It is not only the essence of the product that needs to be conveyed, but the amount of information and experience previously gathered will save time and costs in any new iteration of the product.
4   Are the processes carried out in-house or subcontracted?
    This has implications for the budgets and timelines.
5   What is the relationship between the source market product owners and those in the target market?
    It is important to know the level of involvement the product owners or creators will have in any of the versions of the product elsewhere.
6   Who are the people involved, in what capacity?
    In a production company engaged with a remake or in a platform that brings fans together for free translation, it is very important to know who will be taking part of the process.
7   What is the recognition, compensation and assignment of copyright or IP participation provided to those involved?
    In some cases, adapted formats would be worth selling as finished products to other markets. Voluntary translations or dubbing might be done for free but predicated upon recognition of authorship and attribution or demanding compensation if exploited commercially. This is a central aspect to understanding how the product may be exploited in its original or modified form, and prevent labour abuses and copyright infringement.
8   What elements have been chosen to be modified and how?
    One of the earlier problems with international sales of finished products were that the IP for the dubbing or subtitling belonged to a company different than the one trading the product, which meant rights to use the subtitling or dubbing had to be acquired for further use in markets that use the same language. The same may happen in the case of video games derived from previously dubbed products (check the case of *South Park: The stick of truth* in Uribe-Jongbloed et al., 2016). If there are elements that need

to be added or removed from the original product, this is something that would need to be discussed from the beginning and budgeted according to that.

Although the questionnaire does not address all the questions that might be required for each case, they serve to present the possible discussion points that need to be defined when addressing a cultural transduction. These questions seek to highlight the various aspects that are related to the tenets presented. Some would require to be developed further in historically established markets that already possess legal frameworks that distribute responsibilities, whereas in other cases the novelty of the ways to access markets requires new thinking. As Netflix has shown in the past decade and the recent trend of virtual concerts in multiplayer games highlight, these debates are current and changing constantly, requiring for academic as much as regulatory redefinitions of cultural products and media work (see, for instance, Marino, 2016, 2021; Omidi et al., 2022).

Cultural transduction might be in the realm of those wanting to sell already successful products, or as part of the development of a product itself. It is almost impossible to think of a single system that would consider all possible products, but the openness in the definition of the framework enables for a variety of products to be assessed, recognising the inherent risks in preparing a product for cultural transduction.

It is at this point that a new call to apply, revise, and criticise the framework arises. As a theoretical and pragmatic construct, the framework is still a work in process. It demands further attention from academics and practitioners alike to test its usefulness as a model and as a tool for those involved in these processes. Its shortcomings are surely dependent upon my own lack of expertise or foresight, but they could surely be addressed by those that would engage with it in the future.

## References

Bernal Merino, M. Á. (2016). Glocalization and co-creation. Trends in international game production. In A. Esser, M. Á. Bernal Merino, & I. R. Smith (Eds.), *Media across borders. Localizing TV, films and video games* (pp. 202–220). Routledge.

Bolaño, C. (Ed.) (2012). *Comunicación y la Crítica de la Economía Política*. Ciespal.

Cattrysse, P. (2020). Translation and adaptation studies: More interdisciplinary reflections on theories of definition and categorization. *TTR*, *33*(1), 21–53. https://doi.org/10.7202/1071147ar

Cattrysse, P. (2017). Cultural transduction and adaptation studies: The concept of cultural proximity. *Palabra Clave*, *20*(3), 645–662. https://doi.org/10.5294/pacla.2017.20.3.3

Cuelenaere, E. (2020). Towards an integrative methodological approach of film remake studies. *Adaptation*, *13*(2), 210–223. https://doi.org/10.1093/ADAPTATION/APZ033

Elleström, L. (2017a). Adaptations as intermediality. In T. Leitch (Ed.), *The Oxford handbook of adaptation studies* (pp. 509–526). Oxford University Press.

Elleström, L. (2017b). Transfer of media characteristics among dissimilar media. *Palabra Clave, 20*(3), 663–685. https://doi.org/10.5294/pacla.2017.20.3.4

Elliot, K. (2013). Theorizing adaptations/adapting theories. In J. Bruhn, A. Gjelsvik & E. F. Hanssen (Eds.), *Adaptation studies: New challenges, new directions* (pp. 19–46) Bloomsbury Academic. http://dx.doi.org/10.5040/9781472543349.ch-002

García-Avis, I., & Diego, P. (2018). Perfiles profesionales en la adaptación de series televisivas. *Palabra Clave, 21*(2), 310–337. https://doi.org/10.5294/pacla.2018.21.2.3

Han, B.-Ch. (2015). *The Burnout Society*. Stanford University Press.

Hutcheon, L. (2013). *A theory of adaptation*. Routledge.

Marino, S. (ed.). *El audiovisual ampliado*. Ediciones Universidad del Salvador.

Marino, S. (ed.). *El audiovisual ampliado II. Tradiciones, Estrategias, Dinámicas y Big Data en Argentina*. Ediciones Universidad del Salvador.

Miller, T., & Yúdice, G. (2004). *Política cultural*. Gedisa.

Miller, T., Govil, N., McMurria, J., & Maxwell, R. (2005). *El Nuevo Hollywood*. Paidós.

Murray, S. (2008). Materializing adaptation theory: The adaptation industry. *Literature/Film Quarterly, 36*(1), 4–20.

Omidi, A., Dal Zotto, C. & Picard, R. G. (2022). The nature of work in the media industries: A literature review and future directions. *Journalism and Media, 3,* 157–181. https://doi.org/10.3390/journalmedia3010013

Rohn, U. (2010). *Cultural barriers to the success of foreign media content: Western media in China, India and Japan*. Peter Lang Verlag.

Rohn, U. (2004). *Media companies and their strategies in foreign television markets*. Institut für Rundfunkökonomie an der Universität zu Köln. http://www.rundfunk-institut.uni-koeln.de

Sanders, J. (2006). *Adaptation and appropriation*. Routledge.

Sherry, J. (2016). Adaptation studies through screenwriting studies: Transitionality and the adapted screenplay. *Journal of Screenwriting, 7*(1), 11–28. https://doi.org/10.1386/josc.7.1.11

Szwydky, L. L. (2023). CODA: Transmedia cultural history, convergence culture and the future of adaptation studies. In L. L. Szwydky & G. Jellenik (Eds.), *Adaptation before cinema: Literary and visual convergence from antiquity through the nineteenth century* (pp. 283–303). Palgrave Macmillan. https://doi.org/10.1007/978-3-031-09596-2_13

# Index

Note: **Bold** page numbers refer to tables and page numbers followed by "n" denote endnotes.

84   *Index*

Printed in the United States
by Baker & Taylor Publisher Services